SIGNS OF GLORY

Making Christian Choices

by

Louise M. Des Marais

DIMENSION BOOKS
DENVILLE, NEW JERSEY

First published 1975
by Dimension Books Inc.

To my friend
Avery Dulles, S.J.

"Our willingness to make
the venture of being a Christian
will in great part depend on
whether we can believe that
in renouncing ourselves
for the sake of others,
with full reliance on Christ,
we shall come to our full stature
as persons."

from *The Survival of Dogma*

ACKNOWLEDGMENTS

The author expresses deep gratitude in dedicating this book to Rev. Avery Dulles, S. J., formerly of Woodstock College and now Professor of Systematic Theology, Catholic University of America, whose creative guidance, encouragement and patient evaluation continued throughout the writing of it. I wish also to thank Rev. Henry J. Bertels, S.J. and Rev. Edward S. Dunn, S.J., librarian and assistant librarian of Woodstock College, New York, for facilitating the research. (May I wish them well in their new location, Georgetown University, Washington, D.C.). Thanks are due to Rev. Thomas A. Burke, S.J., Director, Program to Adapt the Spiritual Exercises, who met with me when this book was just an idea, who provided sources, and read portions of the manuscript, particularly chapters pertaining to discernment; to Mrs. Robert Hinshaw and the late Mrs. Sidney Reed, Jr. for their helpful comments; and to my family.

March 7, 1975   L.M.D.

CONTENTS

INTRODUCTION

It is becoming increasingly evident to us that we make or break ourselves and the world we live in by our everyday choices. Mature and responsible choices, which are made with concern for others, have their origin in faith, knowledge and love. But, how often are our decisions so oriented?

I have spent a number of years attending meetings of various kinds: at the United Nations, as a representative for the World Union of Catholic Women's Organizations; as national chairman of the Family Affairs Commission of the National Council of Catholic Women; as Board and Executive Committee member of the National Council on Religion and Public Education; as a member of the National Committee of the Listening-to-Lay People Project, National Council of Churches; as a member of the sponsoring committee of the Yorkville Counseling Center and of other local groups. It is from this body of experience that I would like to speak to the question: *Do we realize the full human dimensions of our individual and corporate decision-making?*

And further: Do we bring to our choices what we are; what we believe? Are we spiritually aware that Jesus is present in whatever time or place we find ourselves, and that he shared with us the risk and sacrifice involved in being human? Do we realize that because and not in spite of our humanity, we have the capacity to become like Jesus and to reach eternal fulfillment according to God's promises? In faith do we seek God in all things and are we open to opportunities for helping to bring about His kingdom?

The specific purpose of this book is to examine the interrelationship between suffering, communion and discernment. Throughout history, it has been God's chosen ones who penetrate the meaning of trends in society and who work against tremendous odds, often involving definite risk and personal sacrifice, to bring about constructive change. They see as the arena, the place in which they work, whether in industry, government, education—at whatever level—and they try to apply their personal and corporate insights to the problems at hand. To them their human activity is conditioned for eternal union with God and blessedness forever, or not.

In our day, experts are making awe-inspiring discoveries in the life-sciences, in industrial technology, in methods of communication and yet, others warn us that we are on the road to decay, that we have lost sight of our goals and are seeking completion in the temporal. As Alistair Cooke describes it: "In this country, a land of the most persistent idealism and the blandest cynicism, the race is on between its decadence and its vitality."[1]

How else can we explain the greedy consumption of the earth's goods and resources? We have been so gadget-happy that we were unhappy if we didn't have an electric carving knife and all other appliances that needlessly consumed electric power. Our love of show and luxury has created a shortage of goods among the poor; it has blinded our vision, so we do not seem to see or understand the extent of malnutrition and disease in our own and developing countries. In our day, there is an obsession with the sexual act as a game, a pacifier for loneliness; we fail to grasp its true meaning—the expression of deep, personal love between man and woman, as they work out their marriage commitment. The media often create shock with brutality and violence. On the other hand, the more obscure an art object, the more we force ourselves to find a meaning. We even take the life of the unborn without considering the grave moral implications.

Along with the acceleration of change in contemporary life, our most basic sources of security—marriage, family and the home—are far less permanent now than they were a few years ago. Their very existence is often challenged. Rapid change was graphically witnessed by returning POWs from the unwanted war. After six or seven years in prison they felt disoriented, alarmed and uneasy about the significance of each new "thing." Does this sudden alienation teach us something about our choices? These men found themselves confronted with a whole new set of values. As we choose, do we stop and consider what is happening long enough to evaluate the quality and effect, short and long-range, on human lives, and, more important, the implications on the soul-growth of persons? Couldn't apathy in this regard lead to the decline of our civilization? Ours is certainly no more immune from destruction through lack of vision, dedication, self-discipline than was the Roman. Every act done without selfishness and done for the universal good is part of maintaining a civilization.

We should ask ourselves, as God's people, if we recognize the importance of living our covenant with God concretely each day. It is His plan that each person be in a certain place at a particular time in history for the purpose of building His kingdom. Shouldn't we take up our work in the world more seriously, with a sense of mission? It seems necessary to periodically assess progress and reasons for lack of movement in the right direction. It seems too that a systematic appraisal of roles, demands and response is indispensable to this growth-movement. If this movement toward completion (which at the same time is our eternal beginning) can happen only within the span of years spent on earth, then conditions in the world affect this total human growth.

We can live the human and divine with Jesus through the particular demands of our lives, demands which for each of us are distinct and yet similar. We will find that a definite effort is necessary to keep faith and hope alive, for peace of soul is difficult to maintain in the contemporary scene. We find plurality of opinion within the Church and among churches and as Karl Rahner points out: we face a dual pluralism, outside ourselves and within ourselves, and because of this we experience a gap between what we are and what we should be; "the wider one's experiential base, the more difficult becomes the task of internal integration."2

We will experience the movement of the Spirit, and therefore peace, if we unite ourselves to Jesus and the will of His Father. In order to do this we strive to know Him and seek the truth. And yet, we are urged into the opposite direction by so many inducements. For instance, the fact of life known as suffering inclines us to become discouraged and depressed. We are tempted to lay the blame on God's will, and yet the Good News of the gospels tells us that because of Jesus, suffering has meaning; it becomes our passage to glory and insight, enabling us to make God-inspired spiritual decisions, rather than self-centered ones. It is our union with Jesus which inclines us to do what is good. If we do good for others, then we can be sure that we do the will of the Father.

Today much time is given to raising consciousness. It is well to realize when something needs to be done, but it is more important still to discern what must be done to fulfill even the most basic human need.

Conditions which are a denial of human dignity, for example, in housing or employment, can be improved only after careful decision-making and creative solutions have been reached, with an awareness of the possible consequences of selected action. Negative acts of greed, for personal gain, seem to break, rather than build.

We are obliged frequently to make important decisions which affect other people's lives, and very often we help shape national and international policy. Within his famous *Spiritual Exercises,* St. Ignatius Loyola stresses the importance of discernment, of knowing how to choose between good and evil inclinations. His method is useful whenever decisions are made personally or collectively. We need to be familiar with this already heralded method of discernment, so necessary is it to the life of the Christian. Up to now it has been used largely by members of religious orders, but it seems essential also to lay persons for making right decisions in the public sector. Within their occupational, political and social roles, they have relationships and responsibilities which give them the power to build or destroy. Though still earthbound, the people of God, ever-seeking a higher level of living, can choose to rise and reach new heights of understanding as they share in the work of the Lord.

Teilhard de Chardin wrote in *The Appearance of Man,* "Faith has need of all the truth."[3] The vibrancy of his thought is familiar to many readers. His awareness of motion and of "becoming," was so real to him that he dedicated his whole life to it. Was he, perhaps, not leading us, a precursor, the very one for whom he asked: "I dream of a new Saint Francis or a new Saint Ignatius, to come and give us the new type of Christian life (at once more involved in and more detached from the world) that we need."4

As we seek the truth through discernment, we will find it inseparable from "the way" of suffering and "the life" through communion. For Christ has said: "I am the way, and the truth, and the life; no one comes to the Father but through me" (Jn. 14:6).

Chapter 1

OUR DYNAMIC SIGNIFICANCE

"People" was the name of a popular song some years ago. It acknowledged our interdependence. This chapter, which will lay the foundation for those that follow, deals primarily with our origins as Christians, as Easter people, who, while engaged in different ministries, share the same mission of helping restore the world to God. Our interdependence, as we work out our Christian lives in the contemporary world will, hopefully, become more and more evident throughout the pages of this book. So will the profound truth of our dependence upon God.

A contemporary theologian writes: "From the Christian point of view the synthesis of God and world, and the concrete integration of the world on its way to God always lie in Christ."[1] Risk, sacrifice and glory, then, are involved in the full integration of persons with God, and in the restoration of the world in which they live. An obedience in love (which becomes obedience in mission, work and suffering) are indicated, for Christ, our model, did the will of His Father through love.

It is not enough to *say* that we are Christian. Unless we make an effort to learn about this distinctive way of life, by hearing or reading the Word frequently, we will not grow in the knowledge and love of living a mystery. We should review and understand our origin, mission and ministries. The vitality and dynamism found in almost any passage of the New Testament assures us that the impact of the Christian in this world can indeed be great. We can't afford to complain that we have heard or read such and such a passage of Scripture before. The full wisdom of the message requires a pre-disposing; a genuine desire to assimilate the deepest significance of truth, so that it may penetrate our whole being. It is never certain just when the revealing will take place, but when it does it brings unmistakable inspiration and peace.

As God's people, let us consider, for a moment, our roles as defined in the New Testament. First of all, *who are we*? We are "chosen ones" and are instructed to "clothe ourselves with heartfelt mercy, with kindness, humility, meekness and patience" (Col. 3:12). We are "learners" and the Messiah is our "teacher" (Mt. 23:8–10). We are "brothers" in Christ, "a community of believers," who are of "one heart and mind" (Acts 4:32). We are "children of God" and "heirs of God, heirs with Christ, if only we suffer with Him so as to be glorified with Him" (Rom. 8:16,17). Jesus spoke to us as a shepherd and called us his sheep (Jn. 10:14-16). We are "fellow citizens of the saints and members of the household

[15]

of God" (Eph. 2:19). We are called "children of light and of the day" (1 Th. 5:5). We are "one body in Christ" (Rom. 12:4,5). We are members of a community, the Church (Col. 1:18). We are "living stones, built as an edifice of spirit, into a holy priesthood, offering spiritual sacrifices acceptable to God through Jesus Christ" (1 Pt. 2:5).

And *what is our mission*? Our mission is to proclaim the works of the Lord, who called us "from darkness into his marvelous light" (1 Pt. 2:9). We are "fellow workers in the service of Christ Jesus" (Rom. 16:3). We are co-workers (1 Cor. 3:9) as we seek to spread the Good News. We are God's "witnesses" (Acts 1:5) wherever we are, in whatever we do. We are "fishers of men" (Mt. 4:19). We are to be "imitators" of God (Eph. 5:1). We have a particular way of dealing with difficulties: "Endure your trials as the discipline of God, who deals with you as sons" (Heb. 12:7). We are one another's neighbor (Lev. 19:18, Mt. 22:39). We are called "blessed" if we seek to make peace with another (Mt. 5:9). We are "leaven" called to animate temporal affairs with the Spirit that is within us (1 Cor. 12:12—14).

Our dependence upon God and our interdependence with one another is carefully enunciated in Scripture: "There is no Greek or Jew here, circumcised or uncircumcised, foreigner, Scythian, slave, or freeman. Rather Christ is everything in all of you" (Col. 3:11). "There is but one body and one Spirit, just as there is but one hope given all of you by your call. There is one Lord, one faith, one baptism; one God and Father of all, who is over all and works through all, and is in all" (Eph. 4:4–6). Our close bond of sharing reveals that "men of every race and tongue, of every people and nation" form the kingdom, are "priests to serve our God" and are destined to "reign on the earth" (Rev. 5:9,10). History provides data about shifts of emphasis on roles during various periods of the Church's growth.[2]

Since Vatican II, collegiality and co-responsibility are viable concepts which encourage dialogue and suggest other options for effecting significant progress in mission through interdependence. We are becoming more and more aware that we are *all* charged with the some mission, which is the mission of the Church: to proclaim God and help restore His kingdom. This is the Father's business and ours. If each of us listens to what the other has learned through God's special favor, we will gain insight beneficial to all in the community of faithful. Then, a totally integrated Church community, whose members support each other, will become fruitful in corporate thought and action.

In our day, our mission demands perseverence, courage, initiative and concentration on the spiritual dimension, as it touches every facet of our lives. This saving mission is described as freeing, as liberation by Pedro Arrupe, S.J., Superior General:

. . .man in his wholeness is to be freed: his heart from
the sin that enslaves (Jn. 8:34), his eye from the
darkness that is incompatible with the kingdom of light
(Col. 1:13), his will from the pride that proliferates itself
so hideously. . .man is to be freed and must help to free
himself from the derivates of the violence of sin, such as
egoism, injustice, ignorance, hunger, nakedness.[3]

This act of liberating frees us to choose right over
wrong, to deal with others in a mature way, to know
light rather than darkness, hope rather than despair,
faith beyond the reaches of doubt.

The saving mission of the Church in the world is
not the business of the "pastors" alone. One com-
mentator of the Vatican II documents says of
"pastors": ". . .it is their 'noble duty' (praeclarum
munus) to 'shepherd (pascere) the faithful,' to guide
and nourish them rather than impose a mere external
governance upon them, to 'recognize their services
and charismatic gifts,' to see whether they are
genuine, above all whether they lead to harmonious
cooperation in the common undertaking."[4]

Avery Dulles, S.J. notes that according to Vatican
II, all members of the People of God constitute the
"teaching church": "Since the Holy Spirit inspires
and directs the whole People of God, public opinion
in the Church can be a true theological source. The
teaching Church and the learning Church, therefore,
are not two separable parts. The faithful as a whole,
and especially those who have scholarly competence

or charismatic insight, participate in the magisterium. Conversely the bishops are part of the learning Church."5

The mission of the Church itself has "the character of a dialogue." This by its very nature implies "a two-way circuit, an exchange of *truths,* with the world," writes Robert Bultot. "Christian thought, which for so long has remained a one-sidedly clerical thought, must henceforward be elaborated by clergy and laity together."6

It is at Baptism, the time of initiation, that we are incorporated into the Church and commit ourselves to do God's saving work. Every baptized and confirmed Christian takes on the responsibility of living in a positive way by affirming God and His goodness, by being open, peaceful and ready to learn, serve and teach. If we are expected to preach and teach, by what we are and do, as well as by what we say, then we can see that spiritual development through prayer and sacrifice is a common responsibility for all of us. There is no place for apathy or excuses here. If in fact our country is engaged in a race between "its decadence and its vitality," then all the more reason to help restore order to the world according to God's plan of creation. We are meant to become involved in controlling pollution and protecting the environment, not because we are afraid of extinction, but because we love God's creation. Obedience presumes knowledge and love, not fear and destruction. Nuclear extinction and exhaustion of resources and moral decadence do not show reverence for life. As a result of a high level of dedication, a certain inner joy, which derives from belief in the transcendent, transforms us. Because of hope in the everlasting peace promised by Jesus, we can meet the challenges of this life in a unique manner. All of God's people can work together in implementing action-plans with the hope of peaceful co-existence between peoples and a revitalization of God's kingdom in time.

In the life of service God wisely assigns to each one of us a special work. "We have gifts," St. Paul writes, "that differ according to the favor bestowed on each of us" (cf. Rom. 12:4–8). This is identifiable by personal talent, inclination, opportunity and the needs of others, or as Yves Congar explains, "it is expressed in the inclinations which an individual gets from his temperament, education and circumstances, in the invitations he receives, expressly or tacitly, from others, and so on."[7]

The "special work" of each person, then, is a specific ministry through which each one can participate in the mission of the entire Church. These ministries are rooted in the character given at Baptism. We have common roles, common mission, but specific ministries. If through Baptism we are members of the Church, then what we do also affects the whole Church and either furthers or retards the coming of the kingdom.

Those whose ministry is formalized by the rite of ordination, desire to reach all who thirst for the fruits of Christ's priestly sacrifice. Presiding at the Eucharist, they consecrate bread and wine into Christ's body and blood, confirming His Presence among us. They teach the Word and "proclaim release to the captives" (Lk. 4:18). They govern the members of the Church with an authority of love. They help others carry out their public ministry within a fragmented society.

To support those engaged in strictly human endeavors, the ordained act as "inspirators," and give the kind of assistance that requires close cooperation in a spiritually-based relationship. They give welcome support as spiritual guides for the purpose of sharing thoughts and ideas which need interpretation, and evaluating inclinations, rather than giving specific direction. Careful consideration of pros and cons in matters for decision and a choice made for the better, becomes mutually valuable through the proper balancing of the spiritual and temporal values which makes for wholeness in each person.

In his book, *New Communities for Christians,* Francis K. Drolet, S.J. defines this specific task in priestly ministry as stating clearly "those principles that concern the purpose and proper use of temporal things." It includes strengthening the lay person "with moral and spiritual aids" for "renewing the temporal order in the spirit of the gospel and the mind of the Church."[8]

It becomes evident quickly that there is no separation between the temporal and spiritual life when we seek solutions for social ills. Worldly issues more often than not take in the moral and religious dimensions. We find ourselves confronted with the need for basic theological and philosophical principles. Vital issues of concern to everyone deserve the combined expertise of persons trained to evaluate objectively all possible solutions. All men and women of faith should have the opportunity for input, even if indirectly, because the whole People of God, clergy and lay, are intended to be responsible members of Church and society. Certainly persons who are delegated to take part in such discussions should have easy access and even a close association with ordained members of the church community.[9] Theologians, particularly, should evaluate for us the "signs of the times," in the light of their expertise.

Former Secretary-General of the United Nations, U Thant, stressed the necessity "to take into account, as far as possible and in an appropriate manner, the benefits of scientific and technological development, so as to be able to assess their advantages and disadvantages in the light of the intellectual, spiritual, cultural and moral advancement of mankind."[10] Frequent discussion is essential for defining specific strategies and refining tactics as we evaluate basic human problems. The Source of all life and the animator of each one of us steals into the discussion, while we engage in selection of priorities.

As we look about us, we become aware of a very broken humanity and see the need and responsibility to heal, to give, and to make whole those who have lost hope. The Greeks recognized the universal dimension: they saw "a thing never in and for itself but always connected with what was greater"[11]—at once individual and universal, personal and communal. Because we are members of a community called the Church, we grow with others as members of Christ's Body and are anxious when another is in ignorance, filled with perplexity (1 Cor. 12:26). A National Committee of the National Council of Churches, when speaking of the role of the church in this regard, put it this way: "We have a faith that can save us. We need a church that can minister to us and through us to the institutions of society. We call upon the Christian church, from its highest councils to its smallest parish, to call lay men and women to an awareness of their part in this crucial need; to help lay people discover the means of impacting all life with faith; and to create within the church a community of love so that believing man may challenge others with a strong faith by putting what they believe in touch with what they do."[12]

In addition we are members of an immediate community (family, neighborhood, city, state) and members of the world community. It does not take long to realize our interdependence within these communities. Think of what happens when there is a strike of any kind, or the simplest shortage. The discontent of some people can be felt by countless others. Most things that we buy represent an interlocking of effort: the idea, production, shipping, distribution, selling, buying. When we realize this interdependence, then we accept and trust. We find that the cooperative action of others brings out the good in us and we understand more fully what we mean to one another. What we choose to do helps to build or retard the growth of members in each of these communities.

We are called upon to make history by living Christ through our specific ministries in these communities. We do not look with indifference upon the world, or the part of the cosmos in which we are destined to fulfill our assignment. Here there is no call for rejection or fleeing from a scarred world, but rather for acceptance and transfiguration. We look upon it with a spiritual awareness, knowing we are involved in a most challenging plan of action: the coming of the kingdom of God in the hearts of men and women, and consequently in the social institutions in which we work. The striving toward the perfection of charity on the part of ordained and non-ordained has a cosmic dimension and is what will restore and sanctify earthly realities.13 When we witness the apathy of some and the confusion in society, we realize that our task is great. It summons "the semi-divine courage which is latent in all of us" and provides the challenge "to risk all that we have for love."14

It will be by our lightness, optimism, courage, gentleness, patience, that we show our belief in the Risen Christ. And as we read in the *Hymn of the Universe*: "To attain to him and become merged into his life I have before me the entire universe with its noble struggles, its impassioned quests, its myriads of souls to be healed and made perfect. I can and I must throw myself into the thick of human endeavor, and with no stopping for breath. For the more fully I play my part and the more I bring my efforts to bear on the whole surface of reality, the more also will I attain to Christ and cling close to him."15

If we see our responsibilities in the light of eternal truths, we can certainly have a hopeful attitude. Strangely enough, in today's world, it is our eternal destiny which gives us a sense of security and permanence. In a highly mobile society, where the disposable is desirable, a spirituality which is both personal and societal, strengthens the whole, because there is certitude and peace among those bound together by common belief. If we accept others, we accept God, the Maker of us all.

In the following chapter a ministry which is very basic to the development of the person and all peoples commands our attention. How often have we viewed *parenthood* as a ministry, and yet, it is indeed that? Let us consider, then, this important work for it shows clearly the relation between origin, mission and ministry.

Chapter 2

MINISTRIES OF FAMILY LIFE

The family is the natural locus for Christian ministry to one another. Husband and wife minister to the other, as the sacrament of love enriches their relationship with divine wisdom and understanding. Parenting, as a ministry within the family, is the conscious effort to help prepare the young child for loving self, others and God. (Because one can be a parent without actually ministering to the profound needs of children, I prefer to use the word "parenting," rather than "parenthood," emphasizing the action over and above the state.) Though fully aware of the importance of other ministries, in this chapter I would like to develop further the significance of actions which take place between the members of a family. When family mores change as rapidly and drastically as they do today, it seems necessary to re-examine this site of Christian ministry and its distinctive responsibilities.

Despite present trends, family members are dependent on one another. The family as a community assumes recognized need and sharing. Its members are bound together by a similarity which necessitates interpersonal relationships and confirms their interdependence. United Nations Secretary-General Wald-heim extends this interdependence to all life, not only human life: "It is important to deal with the great problems that confront the world individually. Population, environment, energy, raw materials, natural resources, health, employment, education, each element is interconnected with the others. These are global problems which require a global response. No nation, however large or powerful, can escape from the fundamental reality of our interdependence. No individual can escape from it."[1]

God's people depend on one another for life throughout life, knowing that all life and love is God. If God is within us then we extend ourselves easily to others. God's love is expansive—it gives life: our acceptance of another person is a way of giving life and the very act of receiving another's love enables the giving of that love.

If it is so that we are dependent on one another then we immediately see the need to know how to communicate. It is essential that we learn how, because the art of communicating the gospel message is another way of giving life, which, indeed, is the task of the authentic Christian.

The facility to communicate at all is acquired and not given at birth. Each stage in life is a preparation for the next. The infant wants to communicate very early and does so with a smile, a cry, a reaching out. The positive response insures further communication and the communion of two persons. Parents can do much to encourage this learning process.

The child of four wants to communicate by telling a tall tale: the greatest drama evolves from a simple incident with imaginary characters and places presented in graphic detail, progressing beyond belief. Yet, we listen, ask questions and stimulate interest with some light regard for validity. Glimmers of reasoning skills soon manifest themselves and religious instruction can begin in earnest.

During the period of adolescence, a young person's ability to communicate increases only if others cooperate by listening, showing interest, by being open; a valuable gift of self to another. In addition to being a means of learning, communication helps to deepen the communion between two persons of the opposite sexes. If young people develop this art, they will be better prepared for the in-depth relationship of marriage, and parenting, its fruition.

The young mother who feels over-burdened by her responsibilities should not hesitate to communicate this to her husband. Though burdened with his own responsibilities, hopefully he will understand and, with ready response, help her over a difficult time. It is not surprising that the problem of communication is the basis of most marital conflict. To be able to state one's mind and have it received and given a response presupposes unselfishness and positive charity in both cases. It is essential at times to evaluate the quality of communication within a marriage, just to be sure that damaging mind blocks are not building a wall between husband and wife. If a couple are at a loss to know the cause of faulty communication and do not seem to be able to resolve their difficulty, then it is wise to get outside help immediately. Destructive emotions can build up causing tensions with serious consequences to the physical and mental health of one or both persons. Marriage and family counseling serves "to open channels of communication, point out alternatives and options and provide guidance."[2]

If we learn to live in the presence of God, we will realize the superb interplay between each person and the other in God's world. We will recognize that every one has a place in the human community and should take that place as God calls each person. Human relations at best are not easy and yet this is life—our growing in maturity with a desire to do well, not solely for ourselves, but for others, and above all for God.

Parenting is viewed by some with great joy, by others as a burden and inconvenience and by still others as a crisis. Parenting, to the Christian, is a divine mandate. The married state in which husband and wife unite, and which is consecrated by a sacrament of the Church, has an ecclesiological as well as sociological significance. Their child deepens this significance. We will see that child bearing and rearing fit into our over-all theme of interdependence and are related to truth and communion.

It is at Baptism that the attending responsibilities are manifest in full. The sacrament itself is assurance that their important work, if undertaken, will be grace-filled. Not only do parents accept the responsibility of raising their child in a Christian home, but godparents, as well, reaffirm these obligations. The participation of godparents is, as it were, a seconding of a motion made. The teaching duty of godparents appertains to the spiritual development begun at the child's baptism. The fact that godparents accept this assignment contributes to the grace of the sacrament. Infant baptism effectively signifies the inherent grace of being raised in a Christian home and community. Each symbol, the water, the oil, the white garment, the light, reinforces the far-reaching effects of this combined ministry: a leading forth out of darkness to the greatness and glory that is Christ.

The "mission" within the family is the same as that of other ministries: to proclaim the good news and celebrate the sacraments—to tell of God and His love and glory. This heralding begins even before a child is born, for it is revealed through the parents' basic attitude toward life itself. They bring to the fulfillment of their mission who they are and what they have within them. One author says: ". . .parents are in an exceptional position, in that their natural authority and their apostolic responsibility coincide, their natural office and their Christian office merge into one. Their responsibility as Christians occurs at the very root of the life and growth of mankind. When they bring a child to birth, they can bring a disciple to birth too."[3] That is why we must not lose sight of the fact that begetting and raising children is a distinct vocation and calls for careful preparation.

Do we have the ability to transmit to our children the word that God loves us and gives life, that He gave us a mind and will to be free to act in full human dignity, that He made us free to choose how we will act, whether we will move forward or backward, become more or less ourselves and what we are meant to become? Do we understand that He made us free to choose whether we hope or not? In this we find ourselves, for "to hope, to be able to hope, to be able to accept the limits of self and reality, to be able to look to the future with realistic anticipation and purposeful striving—this is what it means to be human."[4] It has been said that each child is a new hope for the world. This hope can be realized only if the early years are as they should be. How important, then, is our capacity to radiate by word and example God's love and joy to the young child; for each child bears the seeds of glory.

It is at the very beginning of life that the being and becoming of the religious person is set into motion. "The infants' fundamental faith-shaping experience is associated with developing a sense of trust, that is a perception of the world as a friendly and reliable place in which people intend to do him good rather than harm." Eugene Kennedy continues by saying that Erik Erikson affirms that this is the work of the first year of life and the responsibility and opportunity of the mother.[5] Another person confirms this by saying, "the family is not only a pastoral object but a pastoral subject, wherein the woman has evidently a very important part."[6] It should be noted, however, that all members of the family (mother, father, brothers and sisters) influence the total development of the child, as do other relatives also.

At a meeting of experts convened by UNESCO the participants decided that "the only practical means for promoting the development of the young child is by activities which help the parents to provide more effective child care. In other words, the family is the key to helping the child."[7] A prominent child psychiatrist and pediatrician, who directs the Early Child Development Center in New York City, feels that too much public money is spent on teaching other people to care for children and not enough on teaching mothers how to be mothers.[8] It can be added here that similar activities are needed to prepare parents for providing adequate religious instruction. The family home has long been regarded as a "little church." Measures taken to motivate parents to develop liturgical practices in the home will further contribute to the presence of His glory within the home itself and in the lives of the family members.

Adequate knowledge regarding child bearing and rearing are most important because the child is completely dependent on parents or surrogates for sustaining life. The physical, psychological, emotional and spiritual development of the child is begun by the parents. The initial love-exchange between parent and child begins almost instantly. If it does not take place the over-all development, including the spiritual, is retarded or destroyed beyond remedy. Deprivation, particularly of maternal care, can have lasting effects on the child's personality. The call back to breast feeding is a plea for the natural way of expressing the fundamental attitude of caring. During the formative years parents are called to continue caring by creating an effective learning environment for their children.

The following incident points out that learning experiences happen around the clock. One day on 86th Street in New York City two black women were accompanied by a little white boy and a black girl. The little girl reached for her friend's hand. At first he wouldn't take it. She began to put her arm around his shoulders. Her face had the expression of wanting to extend herself, to reach out in love. Her mother, at that moment, turned and began scolding her. The child began to cry. Her joy was transformed into alienation, rage, anger and sadness. Rather, it seemed necessary to encourage, to build, to bring to brilliance those qualities in the human person which would let her become what she was meant to be—a manifestation of God's glorious love for us. This small event was important in this child's learning experience and no doubt left a lasting impression on her character.

In an article called "Alienation — Context and Complications" the author states: "The crucial question that confronts our society and our religious commitment at the present hour is whether we can eliminate, reject, control, or cure the residues of infantile rage and resentment without at the same time destroying the ideals, values, faith and hope that are the lifeblood of society."9 For love and hate live very close to one another. We have only to examine ourselves to see how quickly hostility rises. If we look into the annals of crime we realize that the acting out of hostility costs lives which might have been spared had the early need for love been met in the criminal. The unwanted and unacceptable can develop feelings of inadequacy and frustration which give birth to continued acts of violence and other irrational behavior. We have only to think of how empty our lives would be, how lonely and hurt we would feel without the love of family and friends. Neglect is destructive. It isolates, hampers growth, alienates one person from the other; it breeds anxiety, anger and produces perverse thoughts. How can a person reach full potential and create work worthy of God, if creativity is stifled for want of love?

It is difficult to understand why, then, the young child's necessary security and self-esteem is fractured for the benefit of economic growth of either person or nation. There is no substitute, in most cases, for the ready response to the natural quest of a young infant to be loved, touched, reassured, enjoyed by the mother. We should remember too that the child also affects the mother. This encounter is fundamental to the continued growth and development of each of them, for one never gives love without there being the possibility of response from the other. If early needs are met, there is a greater chance of realizing an adult who performs and produces responsibly, because there is no need for constant self-interrogation (who am I?, where am I going?, what should I do?) beyond adolescence. The roots of self-acceptance are well-established.

If we approve and reassure, the very young child will grow having a good self-image. A child who accepts self has quiet conviction and confidence in meeting the joys, threats and exigencies of life. This child will enjoy people, but will be able to be alone and will have peace. The child who is unhappy about self will act in quite a different manner: this child will remain isolated, will bully people or will overextend socially, fearing rejection. Interior balance is important not only to persons themselves but to the condition of the world in which they live. Psychologists and psychiatrists seem to agree that when possible every effort should be made to enable this early sharing between child and parents to take place, so as to enhance the formation of character. There is "widespread recognition today that the child's experience in the first years of life very likely determine what sort of adult he will become."[10] We read that consideration for the child's sense of security, sense of belonging to a family group and other emotional aspects of his personality are as important for his future as his cognitive and social development.[11]

We can see how closely interwoven are the various dimensions of child development by reading scripture. We discover that the people of Israel believed that the unborn child's body and soul were fused together by the Lord, who "spreads out the heavens, lays the foundation of the earth, and forms the spirit of man within him" (Zec. 12:1). Jesus had particular concern for the newborn (Mt. 24:19). What do these phrases "I have stilled and quieted my soul like a weaned child. Like a weaned child on its mother's lap. . ." (Ps. 131:2) say to us? The passages in Mark's gospel where Jesus took children in His arms, and put His hands upon them and blessed them are well known (Mk. 9:36,37; 10:14–16). Children are indeed "a gift from the Lord" (Ps. 127:3–5). Such excerpts presume the importance of parental maturity, the value of touch, and the far-reaching effect of acceptance, all of which are declared basic principles for sound psychological development.

[37]

Communications skills are also important to the spiritual life of each member of the family. The interrelationship between life, truth and communion are immediately apparent. Prayer is communication between God, man and woman or child. It is a conversation (but there need not be words) with someone who is special. The Son, Jesus Christ, is our friend, who lived as man on earth and understands. We can feel free to talk openly with Him. We can consider ideas or ponder options and plans. As in any conversation we should be ready to listen and respond, thereby renewing ourselves continually and helping to renew the world.

In a brief but significant book the author writes: "Pray we must, study we must, give we must; but above all we must find our lives bathed in the reality of God's faithfulness."[12] God becomes more and more real to us as we listen to Him. We may feel less and less worthy and able to do His work, but at the same time others will find strength and help from us. If we place ourselves at God's disposal, He will, without delay, through opportunity and circumstance, pave the way for acting out our Christian commitment as parents.

The perspective of authentic Christians, however, should have no geographical, ethnic or sociological boundaries. We should move in the world ready to bring to secular affairs the fruits of living dynamically according to the Word. We should be sensitive to the presence of God in all persons and things and use our talents and energy to enlighten those darkened and saddened lives. As Alfons Auer reminds us: "The spiritual life is not to be lived merely alongside or outside the other spheres of life, for all the aspects of life must be ordered to growth in holiness and an integration in holiness. . . .In every concrete situation in life the Christian layman [laywoman] must be conscious of his [her] partnership with God in the divine plan of creation and redemption."[13]

It is by this close and constant communication that the union of Christ and the Christian who believes, loves, and hopes is established. If we are sincere Christians, we will help each other and our children progress daily towards the authenticity God intends us and them to have. We become other Christs with one another and throughout the developing process, whether in infancy, childhood, middle or later years, we strive to nurture the spiritual dimension of our lives by uniting ourselves to Christ in his suffering, death and glory. Christ has communicated His promises to us. What is our response? Do we respect and love this life, or do we reject it? Are we able and willing to communicate to each other and to our children the glory which is now and will be forever? This is the essence of Christian family life.

Chapter 3

REDEMPTIVE SUFFERING

"One of the principal effects of the Christian life is peace, joy of spirit, and liberty of heart. For, besides the examples of our fathers, which we read or hear recounted, we have in our days, under our eyes, true Christians, whom the tempests and revolutions of this world do not move; who, on the contrary, glory in tribulation, and remain firm and stable in the confession of the faith of Christ. It is necessary, then, for us to seek out the source of these effects, to explain how it happens that the more one is attached to Jesus Christ by holiness, the more the soul progresses in liberty and serenity."[1]

Are these words, which were written by the great Dominican preacher, Girolamo Savonarola, at Florence in 1497, as true today, as they were then? Indeed, our times are filled with unrest, changes and uncertainty, which we must try to live with in order to survive. Even if most of us are not called to weather "tempests and revolutions," and our measure of "tribulation" may not exceed the ordinary sufferings of a quite ordinary life, we can "glory" in them and "remain firm and stable."

It is God's plan that we meet life's experiences the way Jesus Christ did and thereby become holy. What does it mean to choose to suffer as the people of God? Dr. Viktor Frankl found it possible to endure suffering "with honor" for the sake of another. He, who experienced the inhumanity of concentration camps, built a school of psychiatry based on the will to meaning. Those of his fellow prisoners who found meaning in their lives—an experience, event or person—survived the horrors which destroyed others among them. The mental effort under such conditions must have been tremendous, yet, once these prisoners took the initial step and chose to live, the rest seemed possible.

Suffering walks with us throughout life. For example, what was the nature of your latest hurt? Was it a cold shoulder from someone you tried to befriend? Was it an annoying responsibility that ran against your grain? Was it the fact that you had too much to do in too little time? Was it a waiting period, during pregnancy for instance, that you thought would never end? Was it a tooth-ache or bad news from home? Or was it a diagnosis of cancer or the death of a dear one? There are all types of suffering: some loom little, some loom large. At every turn we face suffering: accept or reject it. It is quite evident that if suffering is a fact of life, then it would be well to examine our attitudes toward it. I do not suggest that we relish suffering, but rather that if we wish to live in a productive manner, we should turn the negative to a positive, by discovering the redemptive value of suffering. In this chapter I will attempt to do this, as well as point out other dimensions of suffering.

A basic necessity for the achievement of peace in the face of suffering is the realization that God does not cause suffering. Often suffering is cast in a most cruel form. A young American wife was vacationing in Rome with her husband, who was stricken quite suddenly and in the early morning hours with a fatal heart attack. Because of the language barrier, she could not reach a doctor or ambulance fast enough, nor did the Embassy personnel rush to help her. Her husband died while she and the occupant of the next hotel room tried to revive him. The web of ensuing details: no money to move the body, what to do with his clothes, how to tell the children at home, all intertwined to shape a veritable nightmare. The frustration experienced at such a time is almost unbearable, for our instinct is to save life and yet all circumstances militate against our doing so. There are times, such as this one, which belie the most positive act of trust. What about mistakes made through sheer circumstance, blundering ignorance or insensitive carelessness: the ambulance delayed in a traffic jam, "if he had gone to the doctor sooner," the pay check stolen from a family man, the jealous principal who fires an innovative teacher, victims of political opportunism, civilian casualties during military attack and any number of situations.

At times like these we may ask, "Where is God?" and we may suffer a lack of faith as well. This is precisely when and why we can "throw ourselves naked into His hands, expecting everything from Him."[2] For He is the One who shows us how to bear the crisis of doubt, by giving us adequate grace to see His Son's life in each cross. If we do not accept this grace, we become victims of discouragement, and even despair, and lack the motivation to rise out of grief. The spirit grows in meeting each trial head on. We shall see further on that this growth-movement is beneficial to the individual and can be beneficial to others, as well.

We might say there are two kinds of suffering: *personal* and *corporate*. Personally, we may suffer from failure, lack of acceptance, exhaustion. We suffer physical pain. Friction and frustration are kneaded into our relationships with others. We hurt when we are deprived of the presence of a loved one. We ache to be reunited with family. We have ideals and goals and find them beyond our strength to achieve. We are often beset with temptations and experience "sadness" in the wake of moral weakness. All these are personal, deeply-felt, sufferings.

We deal with *personal* suffering in different ways. Some of us may gripe about it; mentioning it to everyone we meet. Others of us may simply suffer in silence or take our mind off it by becoming interested in something else. At times we are more vulnerable than at others. Usually we take out our aggravation on others or withdraw within ourselves and build up resentments which choke the spirit and make life an unpleasant experience for ourselves and those around us.

In addition to personal suffering, we must bear the burden of the times. We might call this *corporate* suffering. Conflict and violence are the conditions of our day. Most of us suffer financial anxiety because of the high cost of living. We witness decadence in media and seem powerless to change the trend toward materialism, permissiveness and depersonalization. Crowding in cities, inadequate housing, malnutrition, pollution, cause suffering to us as groups of people. Yet, in the midst of all this we are expected to share each other's burdens and even forget ourselves to the extent of overcoming prejudice, jealousy, envy, pride in the process. Not an easy thing to do though sometimes, despite ourselves, we are forced into it by circumstances. Think of the sharing of burdens that takes place at the time of any disaster. In Washington during the riots in the late 1960s, whites who had formally opposed open housing stood side by side with blacks giving food and supplies to those who had lost their homes in the fires resulting from the riots!

Shouldn't we ask what is our role in *causing* both kinds of suffering? Our actions daily reach into the lives of others. If we do good, we shall find that blessings abound and there can be hope and joy in the Lord; but if we do evil, we injure ourselves and others and we offend God. Extensive damage can be brought about by excessive drinking for example. Not only does the individual suffer degradation, but his family are deprived of the support and love they are meant to have. Others than the alcoholic's immediate family may be injured in an accident resulting from excessive drinking.

Or, let us dwell for a moment on a concrete everyday and frequently repeated human condition. An unfortunate marriage in which personalities are incompatible, is fraught with tension, anxiety, hostility and anger. Each of the partners escapes into a private, self-contained world, avoiding friction by minimizing encounters. Is there a call here to love despite a lack of response, which is perhaps due to an inability to love? A union which was meant to grow, but whose growth is stunted perhaps by mental blocks, psychological difficulties or unfaithfulness, is threatened. An examination of the commitment made on the part of each is enough to suggest other possibilities. If the couple cannot agree to seeking counseling could "for better or for worse" mean that there is an opportunity here for one partner to grow spiritually by imitating Christ in His most desperate moments? This would be an example of creative understanding (or "creative fidelity" as Gabriel Marcel calls it) within the married state. If Christ is present in this decision, He will inspire unselfishness, by clearing away weeds which immobilize the will, and He will initiate a sincere desire to do good in the face of apparent neglect. Who else but the Spirit would motivate a partner to continue a difficult marriage? Who else but the Spirit who is love, could release divine energy and suggest that such an oblation could help save a soul for God? On the other hand, a "dead marriage" should be recognized as such before the result of a high degree of imprudence is reached. This point of no return is usually manifest in physical or mental symptoms and suggests the solution of necessary separation. We should perhaps add here that: "Even when stable forms of life fall apart, as in the breakup of a marriage or in the dispensation of religious vows, God will always be at hand to point out another way to walk. Ability, preference, and opportunity are not casual happenings but signs and intimations of God working at the very heart of life."3

Suffering is both individual and universal. We suffer alone, but we soon learn that we are not the only ones who suffer. We are forced, almost despite ourselves, to make good of a bad situation. We cannot stop with self. When we have made peace with suffering, we find we are made aware of the sufferings of others. We are more vulnerable, but more important, we are more sensitive to the needs of others. As long as another suffers we now know we have the responsibility to move beyond self, to reach out and build community by sharing our faith and hope with that person. It is not so easy to sympathize with another when the spirit is broken by discouragement and despair. It takes great sensitivity to detect such a condition and to determine whether one should try to penetrate "the front" put on by the victim.

Pain, loneliness and feelings of inadequacy are part of the human condition. So many elderly in urban areas are lonely because they are separated from their loved ones. In the great march toward independence, we forget how necessary we are to other people and of our interdependence, the recurring theme of this book. If alert, one can assure a neighbor that another person loves and cares. This compassion is likely to motivate the other to see worth in self and enable that person to rid self of defeating self-pity and to move outwardly towards others. If another has caused us suffering, we must do as Christ did: forgive and forget, care about and for those who injure us (2 Cor. 5–11).

Detachment is a dimension of suffering. The greater our detachment, the more united we are to God in our suffering. We are not devastated when seeing one we love suffer, because we see this as part of the overall interrelationship between the person, Jesus Christ, and the person we know. This does not imply that we do not care about the person who suffers or who has died, but it indicates a realization that this person is a child of God, who is a munificent Father and wills to be united to this human being in a special way. We may be very repulsed by the outward signs of an illness, but we see in it a chance for the great assimilation and integration of two persons who mean to be united in this world and in the next. Other-mindedness, looking beyond self, was understood by Dag Hammarskjold in this manner: "When man's attention is directed beyond and above, how strong he is with the strength of God who is within him because he is in God. Strong and free, because his self no longer exists."[4] If at times of sorrow, we try to forget ourselves, then we are capable of extending the hand of hope and revive belief in eternal and joyful union.

Suffering is a call to self-discipline. A lack of selfishness is at the basis of self-discipline and therefore requires a positive effort. Anne Morrow Lindbergh in her second introduction to *Hour of Gold, Hour of Lead* writes of meeting her own tragedy: "The tradition of self-control and self-discipline was strong in my own family and also in that of my husband. The people around me were courageous and I was upheld by their courage. It was also necessary to be disciplined, not only for the safety of the child I was carrying but in order to work toward the safe return of the stolen child."[5] In her desperation she found it possible to reach beyond her immediate loss to another life which was yet unborn. (I read these words within days of reading this headline: "Abortion Rate 2-1 over births," *New York Post*, August 28, 1973!)

Self-discipline causes us suffering, but at other times it helps us to bear suffering. Though within it there is an element of suffering, it is part of the forward movement as a person becomes truly human. It can be present in the smallest effort like knowing when not to disturb someone, or when not to throw cold water on another's idea. It's knowing when to listen without getting a word in, because this particular person needs someone with whom to talk out a crisis. It's consoling the bereaved; it's doing without to give to another. It's denying oneself certain material goods despite constant bombardment from commercials in the media. It's not hating, not sowing seeds of discouragement through prejudice, not stifling a generous impulse, not hurting others through neglect, not stunting the growth of children through non-acceptance. Definite periods of self-denial have been removed from Church calendars so that these actions may be done in secret, and known only to self and God. This transcendental dimension in our lives should enable us to carefully select the right action in a given situation. If we offer all with love, and therefore "with honor," we grow stronger, and our strength becomes visible to others, and they will ask where we find our strength (2 Th. 3:3).

Clearly our world and its condition points to a need for greater restraint on the part of everyone. There is definite responsibility for all of us to consider others as we make use of the world's resources. We hear much discussion about the quality of life. We noted in the previous chapter that if we do not move in the direction of self-control in some areas of living, the earth as we know it will become more and more polluted. We seem to forget that our greatest asset in the search for better conditions is within ourselves, for self-discipline is the foundation to the development of the whole person. We do not see it as eliminating personal freedom, but rather as enabling us to make better choices, living on a higher plane, "to will a meaning." All that we do should be measured against the greater good. This will very often involve risk and sacrifice, but isn't it true that by our lack of self-discipline we inflict pain on others; such as through greed, anger, pride, promiscuity? The thrill of a few brief moments in illicit sexual activity is self-gratifying, but what does it say of our respect for life in another? As Dom Aelred Watkin writes in his book, *The Enemies of Love*: "To be kind always and on every occasion is an asceticism which, though it does not display itself in some tremendous act of renunciation, demands constant self-control and thought of others."[6]

Self-discipline requires a day-to-day conquering of self for the sake of others, but most of all it is a positive living out of the commitment made at the time of Baptism, to be a new person, and begins in the early years. Even to wait one's turn will teach a child self-control. Though it may cause some pain, at the same time it will strengthen the youngster to face major difficulties later.

To emphasize this important point, we note here that in Secretary General Waldheim's report to the United Nations on Crime Prevention and Control, he stresses the need "to begin with the forms of care and character development which flow from infancy through childhood and adolescence."[7] We have seen in the previous chapter that anger grows out of resentment and the external expression of repressed anger is violence which can result in crime. The interplay between persons increases or decreases the possibility of acceptable or nonacceptable social behavior and therefore the possibility or not of suffering. There is suffering in every crime committed: loss of life, reputation, physical handicap, loss of property. There is suffering even before crime takes place, for crime is often the result of deprivation: spiritual, emotional and physical.

A few words should be said about the suffering of separation from a loved one, though it has been touched upon earlier. It can be a very painful kind of trial. There is a rhythm here, a seeing and not-seeing. The touch and concern of one another unites the two until the next encounter. Could it be, however, that in order to appreciate one another, there is a need for separation? If we did not separate we would not be able to contrast this sadness with the joy of reunion and sharing. We might ask if this does not indicate to us the impact of separation from God by sin and why when reunited to Him by grace we are filled with a joy beyond containing. During the absence of another we are surprised to find that the bond transcends the physical and we remain together in spirit even though separated. The saints have written that even in periods of aridity they have been conscious of God's presence though they knew Him mostly by His absence. The pain of separation can teach us many things!

Perhaps the most significant aspect of suffering is its relation to discernment. Discernment, as a step toward decision-making, so carefully described and developed by St. Ignatius Loyola in his book of *Spiritual Exercises*, consists of "Rules for in some degree perceiving and knowing the various motions excited in the soul; the good, that they may be admitted, the bad, that they may be rejected."[8] Why discernment is necessary is stated clearly by St. Paul: "Our battle is not against human forces but the principalities and powers, the rulers of this world of darkness, the evil spirits in regions above" (Eph. 6:12). I shall give greater attention to discernment in Chapters 6 and 7 of this book, but for now let us consider its relation to suffering.

Couldn't we say that through suffering we gain insight into a quality of spirit? In suffering there is a probing into the significance of the person, life and future life. If we cannot accept suffering, then we cannot expect to reap its benefits. It is not suggested that we enjoy suffering, nor that we not try to prevent or alleviate it, but that when it does exist we use it and not waste it.

Suffering is an important link in the growth process, which if eliminated would negate the grace-power which comes to the one who suffers and the one who consoles. This "death" is part of the movement toward fulfillment, part of the potential, part of the process toward union with Christ. Teilhard de Chardin could see the pain of every "diminishment" or "death" as an act of communion.[9]

Paul was a wise teacher and saw that, "We know that affliction makes for endurance and endurance for tested virtue, and tested virtue for hope"(Rom. 5:3,4). Paul sees Christians suffering as Christians, rejoicing in their trials: "When we suffer and no longer know why, when we suffer without rejoicing, then we are outside of the genuine Christian experience. That is a simple test."[10] Why is it so? Because "the Christian suffers in union with Christ." And beyond the suffering, there is glory which he shares as well—the glory of the Risen Lord. As another author points out: "The resurrection hope readies one for a life in love without reservation." So we then find our identity not "in remaining isolated. . .but only in going out of [ourselves] and becoming personally, socially and politically incarnate."[11]

It is the Christian faith, a grace-gift, that enables us to penetrate the significance of suffering, to unravel the confusion it causes, and rest peacefully in the understanding that with a certain dedication, of it some good will come. Our hope is realistic and transcendent. We do not fear suffering, because, as Avery Dulles, S.J., affirms in his book, *The Survival of Dogma*: "The Christian has no need to shrink in fear from the prospect of poverty, disgrace, captivity, physical pain, apparent failure, even death. None of these eventualities dejects him because he has been taught that to share in Christ's sufferings is the normal way to prepare oneself to share in his glory."[12] "Sufferings and hardships endured in the right spirit keep us young," said a prisoner interned in Siberia for eight years. "It is fear that ages a person—fear of loss, of aging, of failure. . .We must not be afraid of change, of difficulties. Something concrete happens to you when you go ahead with trust in God."[13]

The Christian hopes because of God's promises. Christ's death and resurrection are a guarantee that at the end God's kingdom will be and: "He shall wipe away every tear from their eyes, and there shall be no more death or mourning, crying out or pain, for the former world has passed away" (Rev. 21:4). We believe this despite the opposition that we face now, which at times seems so overwhelming. Today we are pressured into living for the *now* and are made to forget that we live now *for later.* But if we say "I believe" when faced with today's crosses, we give a mere toothache or just being tired a far-reaching significance. Large or small, no burden need be wasted. If we unite our suffering with Christ, then we know that it has redemptive value. Faith and hope prove that there is first a love which accepts an essential condition as being permitted by God for a reason.

Dr. Paul W. Brand, who spent time during World War II operating on men handicapped and disfigured by tragic injuries, concluded a lecture given in Oxford, England in 1963 to the Christian Medical Fellowship during the Annual Conference of The British Medical Association with these words: "With the acceptance of the discipline of pain, suffering for one another, will come also the ecstasy of shared happiness and of a new understanding as we glimpse the vision of God for His own world." Through pain he says we are "called into some kind of mystic fellowship with one another and with our Creator." With deep insight he points out that as the cells of the body had "to suffer with one another before effective multicelled organisms could be produced and survive," so when one man suffers, others suffer community. The same Designer of cellular activity intended that the human race "move on to a new level of community responsibility, to a new kind of relationship with one another and with their God."14

The Christian finds in the person of Christ the model of courage, forgiveness, direction, purpose, faith, power and wholeness while suffering. Through suffering, then, we can reach our full stature as images of God. We feel pain acutely, we face it squarely and accept it in the name of Christ and for His purposes. We experience deep consolation and genuine hope, rejecting the morass of discouragement and despair. We venture to say we might see suffering, as did Teilhard de Chardin, as "a visit and a caress of God." it is at such times that we gain insight—even a well-spring of direction—because the mind is made clear and the will made firm. Is there not, therefore, reason to rejoice?

Chapter 4

SHARING THE JOY OF CHRIST'S PRESENCE

The Eucharist is the central action in the life of the Christian. This Risen Christ-life, received sacramentally, is essential to God's people, because it gives us the quality of life we are called to transmit to others. It is because of our joy in our Lord's continual presence that we can love and serve others and it is this aspect of the Eucharist which I would like to emphasize as we proceed through this chapter. Indeed, our task is the perfecting of ourselves through love, that the divine may be seen in us; for as Pierre Teilhard de Chardin explains: "It is impossible to love Christ without loving others (in proportion as these others are moving towards Christ), and it is impossible to love others (in a spirit of broad human communion) without moving nearer to Christ."[1] When we receive and give Christ in love, we are at peace. Christ living in us is a dynamic synthesis of human and divine energy and activates thoughts and decisions beneficial to others in the community of mankind. In this chapter we shall note the effects of presence—both human and divine—how it can bring joy, stimulate creativity, how it unites, fosters corporate insight and decision.

We interrelate with one another within the family, for example, and this love-exchange contributes to the over-all growth of each person within the family. We know also that discord among family members (beyond the normal amount) has far-reaching effects with sometimes disastrous and permanent results. For example, family meals (if they exist at all) are often hurried, interrupted, or even fraught with tension because of unresolved misunderstandings between some of the persons present. Under such circumstances only a semblance of sharing takes place. The deep-down communication which permeates the saying of grace together is beneficial only if peace is made among us.

The family meal is not unlike the sharing of His Presence in the Eucharist which unites us around the table of the Lord. Depending on the measure of faith, this mystery of the Eucharist can permeate our lives in such a way that at times we are immersed in hope. When we share Christ's Body and Blood, He reaches into the depths of our being and becomes a part of us. He envelops us with His love in the most creative act. As a result, we have a sense of growing stronger, we desire to be and to do, we are encouraged, we know then who we are—we have an unmistakable identity. We become aware that without this close union with Christ we cannot hope to divinize the world.

At a time when apathy and powerlessness seem to

have taken hold of many of us and when events become history before we have read the complete story in the morning newspaper, we do well to look further into the possibilities of divine energy, which can transform us into dynamic and productive persons, which however does not preclude reflection and careful discernment. If we consider the Eucharist the central action in the life of Christians, indeed "our daily bread," then we become absorbed into this action by being prepared in conscience, disposed to receive grace and responsive to Christ's love and promptings. We become more and more persons of *faith* united with the Christian community, both present and absent. We are charged with *hope* and select goals and determine strategies which shake us out of complacency and move us into the areas of universal need. We become a people living among others affecting their lives and those of the totality of mankind, present and to come. We are united to Christ and, therefore, *become supportive of one another, redeeming one another.*

Perhaps to grasp more clearly the effect of Christ's Presence in our lives, we might—however feebly—attempt to make the comparison with the effect a deep and abiding friendship has on us. "Friendship" has been defined as "an attitude that unites two persons of the same or different sex in mutual feelings of admiration, respect, affection and deep tenderness. Its development follows in the wake of growing intimate knowledge and the continuous quiet sharing of all the friends have and are."2 What do we know of the stimulus given by a friend just having shared a moment of precious time in listening? What do we know of the encouragement of a friend, who criticizes objectively, giving an opinion to help us make a decision? Our step is lighter, the sky brighter and the impossible seems possible once again!

Genuine friendship is free, it is open. Friends listen to one another, are grateful to one another, suffer with the other and rejoice together. Friends think of ways to please one another and even surprise each other. Friends keep in touch; they understand when another is weary or discouraged and stand by with needed support. In his book, *The Ways of Friendship*, the late Ignace Lepp writes: "If friendship is to transpire between two people, it is important that both be in a state of availability."3

The Eucharistic encounter is a special moment with a friend, who is our beginning and our final end. A deep and meaningful friendship with Christ is possible; but so much depends on how available we are to Him. He made us for Himself, but left us free to choose whether to accept His overtures of love. He never removes His love—no matter how inhuman we become. He waits and watches while we experiment with pride flaunting our independence by neglecting to seek His help and guidance. He waits, watches and even permits events to happen to us which strip us of our defenses and send us running to Him as a wounded child. We are dependent on Him and He prefers it this way.

The question is: are we conscious of Christ in the Eucharist being our close friend? Do we seek every means to communicate with Him as we do with our closest friend on earth? His presence in our churches is often ignored other than for the liturgy of the Word and the Eucharist, and yet just as we seek out a friend or counselor for advice, we can move toward the Risen Christ in the Blessed Sacrament to talk and listen, even though He is part of our very being. St. Ignatius Loyola once said that no matter how difficult his problems, he always achieved serenity after 15 minutes of prayer before the Blessed Sacrament. So, too, we may come away refreshed, thoughts unmuddled, direction clarified and more fully aware of His presence among us.

When things are not going well in human relations does the power given to us by the sacrament of love enable us to overlook differences? Is it an accident that after the Eucharistic liturgy we have the facility to forget the grudge or the remark said yesterday that didn't sit well, or the sheer dislike of a person? Is it chance that we spontaneously overlook past grievances and willingly try again in a particular relationship? When we are warmed by the Spirit, our difficulties no longer seem insurmountable. The Eucharist, therefore, gives a direction of forgiveness, of reconciliation to our lives.

As God's people united in the body of Christ our forgiving becomes a manner of giving life. We act both individually and corporately in rebuilding lives damaged by wrong-doing. We sow hope where there is despair by tailoring our giving to the need, rather than to what we feel we want to give. We know how miserable, tense and irritable we feel when two among us are not on speaking terms. The strain can become unbearable. The Eucharist inspires us to be the first to move away from self and toward the other.

The grace of the Eucharist directs us away from negative to positive reactions and despite ourselves we begin to contribute. We love more easily because it enables us to do so: "the joy of Christ is reflected and refracted in a thousand encouraging words, friendly gestures, unselfish actions of generosity."[4] We are at the disposal of the disadvantaged, the handicapped, the physically and mentally ill, because we have made ourselves available to God. Not all of us are called to serve in the same manner, however each one of us knows moments in which to make good. No day passes without an opportunity to forgive.

The direction of forgiving and reconciling we suggest, presumes a quality of caring. Though it is not within the scope of this book to develop the importance of caring, mention is made again here that when the psychological crisis between trust and mistrust is resolved in infancy, there is fertile ground for the growth of faith and hope in others, and ultimately in God. Rollo May cites how essential this early experience is: "Care is a state in which something does *matter*; care is the opposite of apathy. Care is the necessary source of *eros*, the source of human tenderness. Fortunate, indeed, is it that care is born in the same act as the infant. Biologically, if the child were not cared for by its mother, it would scarcely live out the first day. Psychologically. . .the child withdraws to his bed corner, withers away, never developing but remaining in a stupor, if as an infant he does not receive mothering care."5 How could such a person be expected later to engage in the process of reaching out, moving toward the world of peoples, seeking to affect others or even the inanimate world, and opening himself to be affected by others; giving shape by relating to the world or requiring it to relate to him?

The person of the Risen Christ, who is present in the Eucharist, raises us to the easy perception of His presence in all things: in persons we meet, events and even in thought itself. We assess better the happenings in our lives when we unite ourselves with Him in faith and begin to understand and realize the plan which God, the Father, has for each of us individually and as members of His people. We know that the Father has sent us as He sent His Son and we have a divine purpose in living.

The generosity of distribution which our Lord

devised represents the attitude of giving we need to cultivate in this life. In Him we have a generous, expansive and, as my husband and I heard Pope Paul VI describe it when addressing Pax Romana delegates in 1971, we have an "explosive" love. We accept, listen to and communicate with one another, whether of different race, religion, nationality, or social class. If our love is not returned and perhaps not accepted, we move then into the realm of sheer giving, which loving an "enemy" takes, though made easier by a moment of grace. It means when there are differences, love erases them, restores peace and order, generates justice as we bear Christ to others and find Him in others.

What more can we say of presence? What more can we say of the power of Eucharistic love? Through our contact with others we grow. This growth is not accomplished in a few weeks. It is part of the on-going process. Human relations at best take careful nurturing with periods of more or less promising fruit. It takes time, just as the seed must germinate, grow roots, have frequent watering and sun before the plant can produce a full bloom.

The Eucharist is an invitation to grow spiritually. This soul-growth process is set in motion at the time of our Baptism, when we die to sin and glory in God's presence and greatness, taking on some of the characteristics of His Son, Jesus. It continues throughout life as often as we respond to the grace-moment of encounter. Though it is disillusioning to see how easily we fall into our old ways after having received the God of life, we shouldn't be surprised, as this is part of becoming a whole and a completely human person. As long as we try—and there is struggle involved—God is pleased. The rising again after a fall is the telling characteristic of those who seek to imitate Jesus, who fell three times under the weight of the Cross. He showed us how to rise again after sin, and move forward in His purifying act of love. Thus we grow in personality and competence with Christ, because we put on "that new man created in God's image, whose justice and holiness are born of truth" (Eph. 4:24).

The Eucharist, the sharing of the divine life, enhances health, but more, it makes us whole. We know His presence, because we actually feel it. The joy we feel is but a shadow of eternal joy. The peace we know deeply within ourselves will be ours never to be taken from us, for we are already partly set, by faith and the sacrament, in the eschatological era.

Let us think for a moment what love of another does for us. Our heart is warmed, skips a beat, our eyes glow and we wish to express the joy in some way: with a hug, a kiss, a gift, a dance or some creative act. Love enables and begets greatness. Think then of what divine love can do to us. We no longer dangle, at sixes and sevens, at odds with ourselves, unsure, afraid. We have an integrated feeling, as if Christ walks with us, breathes within us, puts words into our mouths. We are in complete control and safe. Is this what the Lord meant when He dispelled fear? In the life of the Christian, there is only room for *alleluias*.

Yet, despite reason for rejoicing, we are still saddled with the weight of our times and find the most prevalent tendency today is to think negatively. Tendencies generated by worthy reception of the Eucharist can enhance our whole mental outlook: self-forgetfulness, understanding, tolerance, humility, generosity, honesty, compassion, patience, gratitude, faith, hope, love, acceptance of reality bring happiness, joy, energy, laughter, responsiveness, warmth, peace of mind, optimism, usefulness, adjustment, purpose. The following mental attitudes: self-pity, resentment, anger, defiance, intolerance, false pride, selfishness, greed, indifference, dissatisfaction, impatience, fear, self-hate, envy, disdain, blaming others, reap depression, anxiety, guilt, remorse, insomnia, irritability, tension, loneliness, withdrawal, abuse of loved ones, psychosomatic illness, suicidal and homicidal tendencies.[6] Our impact as Christians, alive with Christ, on the society in which we live will be the mark made by positive living and thinking.

If we realize that Christians live and relate daily with others, and are "involved in the web of events and situations" with definite obligations to influence their future direction, we will understand why it is important to reflect on suffering as a part of everyone's life (which we have done in Chapter 3), the Eucharist as the central act in the Christian's life (which we are now doing) and discernment and decision-making with the effort to do God's will (the subject of the next chapters). The following quotation from a letter of Teilhard de Chardin to Jeanne Mortier, June 20, 1952 emphasizes the relationship which I am attempting to develop:

> Yes, I hope that the Lord will use us as much as possible in the great task of bringing "the Christ of Today" to the world of today. I was thinking again this morning of the profound difference that divides the two ways of understanding both "the heart" and "the Cross" of Jesus. You can see it simply as a suffering "Heart" to be "consoled." Or you can see it as a centre of energy that creates and drives the world: it suffers, indeed, but it is even more a fire, the only fire that can keep in motion a universe that has become reflective.[7]

The relationship is useless unless we are motivated to act on our decisions.

The demands in our daily lives vary as each person moves through the different stages of life. This is clearly evident within marriage and family. The rate of growth is not the same for both partners. The reaction to the death of a child can traumatize one. A communications gap widens and if not checked and dealt with almost immediately can result in future estrangement one from the other. Present mobility can cause frequent job changes and, therefore, uprooting and unhappiness, and a loss of security, even though financial benefits improve.[8] Adolescent children will withdraw from religious practice and puzzle parents into thinking they are failures; that their best efforts have been in vain. But as Father Dulles points out the quality of faith changes with age: "The faith of the child is spontaneous and unreflective. . . .At the stage of adolescence, the critical faculties awaken. . . .A mature faith is one that has overcome the superficial enthusiasm of youth as well as the naive credulity of the child. . . .A mature faith is humble enough to criticize its own presuppositions and learn from the science of its day. By continually dying to its own previous formulations, faith plunges even deeper into the mystery of God."[9]

Other factors, such as illness or accident, bring different and difficult demands on time and energy and morale. They may require a curtailment of previous pursuits, if they involve the care of another person. The victim concerned may be unable to continue work, and will need to adapt to a new situation. The suddenly blind, for instance, must relearn how to do the simplest tasks. It is inspiring to see some so afflicted grapple with adjustment with the optimism of an adventurer.

It is evident then, with the changes that occur

within a lifetime, that as Christians we are obliged to evaluate periodically and systematically whether we are progressing in living the Christian life.

At a time when we all seem to be re-establishing our identity, we might ask if our dedication to a certain way of life still operates as motivation to carry out its responsibilities, or have circumstances reduced ardor, changed the intensity of desire, become a noose to personal freedom? Have we perhaps decided to change from one commitment to another, because it seemed that by doing so one was more faithful to God's designs, and what brought about the change? Has fidelity to our family and friends been sullied by misunderstandings? Faithful in other responsibilities and duties, do we fail to make time to remember the handicapped, the hungry, the ignorant, the lonely, even if only in our prayers? When called upon to state our position on political issues, do we give way to expediency or stand firm in defending human rights?[10] Do we realize we have a duty to enunciate principles which build society as a wave of self-destruction seems to almost overtake us?

In the course of time our world is abused by many evils and "it is the layman, whose life is so thoroughly involved in these institutions [within the public sector], that the challenge of renewing them is primarily given."[11] We cannot live or work with other people very long without becoming quite aware of the conflicts within ourselves. Our own weaknesses are evident when we are direct or indirect parties to oppression, violence, discrimination. However, with purpose, direction and motivation given to us through the channels of grace, we can hope to love rather than hate, do good rather than evil. The law of Christian love "inspires modern man to be responsible for their world, through a spirituality aimed at building a better world. It offers an authentic vision of world development as an essential component of Christian holiness."12 A penetrating sacramental life and the practice of daily personal prayer is essential to such a commitment. This Risen Christ-life received in the Eucharist is necessary to any Christ-work.

Johannes B. Metz describes our duty to be the following: "We must interpret love, and make it effective, in its societal dimension. This means that love should be the unconditional determination to bring justice, liberty, and peace to others."13 As we do this what is happening is a *becoming* and a *coming*. As we read the "signs of the times" we see that our world needs further building and many of us need further humanizing in accord with the designs of our Creator. We cannot lose sight of the fact that every moment of our day is important even the moments of sleep when we rest in the secure arms of the Shepherd.

This is the way of life of the people of God. We are a people of faith and love, who are not fearful even if our God remains silent for a time: "Your love has hidden itself in silence, so that My love may reveal itself in faith."[14] If we have faith, we know that He loves, for He is the source of that faith. The deepest human love we experience teaches us something of the intensity of God's love for us. We know that an authentic love for another which we experience deep within ourselves includes trust and faith and hope that the other loves also. If we are true to ourselves we move with this pulsation of genuine love which is Christ. Eucharistic love transforms us into what we are and will be for all eternity, for Christ-love is transcendent and eschatological. It is our present and our future. How could we risk not loving Him and others with Him?

The Risen Christ gives Himself to us as a pledge and foretaste of our eternal life. By receiving the Eucharist we know at once the present and future which is fully realized in Christ. "By this sacramental contact," one author says, "we enter in a mysterious way into this present moment of salvation realized, and we truly share in it."[15] The Eucharist is Christ, and therefore the greatest influence in our lives. He is within us, part of our being, as we do our work in the world. It is as if through us He accomplishes His plan. The reality of His presence is a mystery. Through worship, works are permeated with the certainty which accompanies the determination to do God's will. Insights into the divine purpose come to us through others, but also directly from Him. St.

Ignatius Loyola concluded repeatedly his correspondence by praying that God would "grant us the grace always to know His most holy will and perfectly to fulfill it."[16] It is in the reality and presence which is the Eucharist that His will is made know to us and grace given to us to discern how best to fulfill it.

Chapter 5

WHO AND WHAT INFLUENCES OUR DECISIONS?

If as we said in the previous chapter we are involved in the web of events and situations with definite obligations to influence their future direction, then we should consider the importance of decisions. No decision is inconsequential. Even the minor and instantaneous decision to listen to or reject a child's questions may have lasting psychological significance. Major decisions require adequate reflection and dedication. Usually decisions involve other people. Therefore, it is important to determine to whom we should give priority, ourselves or others. As people of God we know that prayer should precede and be a constant part of decision-making. Prayer insures more dependable motives for action and gives an amount of certainty that the intent is an unselfish one. However, we shall discover the need for definite rules for discernment in making important choices.

Our decisions vary according to our roles. There are decisions we make within our life commitment as man and wife, father and mother, clergy or religious, unmarried professional. A mother, for instance, makes everyday decisions as a homemaker, consumer, nutritionist, economist, and psychologist, when she buys food for her family. She is bombarded on all sides with suggestions to buy certain products for the premiums received and for the multiple vitamins they contain and, therefore, must choose carefully. Or, if a legislator chooses not to compromise his principles, he may find that his decision affects his political career and family in a negative way. Or, an employer might hire the least promising of three applicants for an office job, because this person needs reassurance and a means to support her family after the death of her husband. We find that each one of these decisions, made within an established role, affects others.

Simple decision-making should begin early in life. Offering simple choices to children is a way of recognizing their individuality. Choosing between a red or blue dress to buy or wear is decision-making in the embryonic stage. However, if the development of the power of reason is allowed to begin early, children will learn to evaluate possibilities and, as mature adults, will accept the consequences of their decisions. It is the right of children to grow with a capacity and understanding for making decisions. At an early age they can discover and consider other persons as an integral part of their decisions.

From our beginning God is at work in us, bringing about our perfection. His plan is that we grow to be like Him, walk in His presence, and work with Him as He prepares us for eternity. It was at Baptism that we agreed to cooperate in redeeming the world. Simultaneous with redeeming is becoming. There is at once creation and incarnation. He wants us to live with "love, joy, peace, patience, kindness, goodness, fidelity, gentleness and self-control" (Gal. 5:22). This, God's plan, can influence our decisions.

If we are aware of the presence of God and commit ourselves to a life lived according to His plan and purposes, our decisions, individual and communal, help bring about the visions of God's kingdom. God present in the world leads us to see how, individually or collectively, we are responsible for the good or harm which insures or upsets the peace we are meant to have. He adds a dynamic dimension and real value and vitality to day-by-day living.

God is with us as the Son. His message in the Gospel, the Good News, is the Word Himself communicating with us at every turn in our lives. The invitation is there for talking, sharing, deciding, if we will only listen. As Michel Quoist, who devotes a whole book to the subject *Christ is Alive!*,[1] says, it is Christ in our lives who makes us live. If we do not recognize and acknowledge His presence then our lives are less full, less meaningful as we move about in our world. He is immanent and transcendent. God, immanent in the world, communicates daily with us to bring about our growth and perfection. He is our present and our future. He draws us up away from despondency to hope, trust and a joy of living.

Linking our purpose to God's forms a bond strong enough to prevent the further disintegration of society and improve the quality of life for all men.

God's people can have a most challenging life, if they are transformed by the light and power emanating from the person, Christ. This power is not loud, but contained and somewhat invisible, though it causes the distinguishable "glow" of Christ present in us. We become animated, more effective. Of paramount importance is our concern and participation in God's plan to bring about the kingdom. If we realize the importance of each decision as contributing to the kingdom, we continue to possess this power. It is a power which makes us free to act in a magnificent way, to come to a penetrating knowledge of truth, and to share in the greatest life.

We have seen in a previous chapter that God's people are a people nurtured on love. This love becomes part of self. Can we realize how God the Father is in the Son by knowing how the love of another becomes part of self? A person would not be as he is, if he were not loved by the other. Acceptance of love *enables* one to love. Because we are loved by God, we are capable of loving. It may help to remember this as we make decisions which affect many people either on a local, national or international basis. We think and work together, not to agree always; rather, to love and work as the servant Church for the good of all. Our task is to help liberate the world from the blight of sin and selfishness. We may find a distinct apathy retards good works on the local level. Or, we may see rivalries build up and prevent results.

A program for the aged, for instance, fumbled at an early stage because the no. 2 person couldn't bear to be no. 2. Actually, she was better qualified to serve in second capacity. Or, it could be that no. 1 is too authoritarian and the others are rebellious and unco-operative. There is no room for selfishness in the Christian who seeks to bring about constructive change. The dedicated Christian makes a love-choice, sweeping away the dust which settles so easily, clouding our vision. One author tells us that "true dialogue, true personal relationships require the courage to make oneself present to the other." He continues, "There are many subtle ways to refuse this presence." He explains that this presence must be renewed often, "a risk that must be repeatedly taken."[2]

If we encounter in another person a spiritual poverty which spawns a negative, withdrawn attitude toward others, are we not obliged to help restore that person's ability to love, to give, to be useful and productive. How much love and understanding is there among the employees of our bank? How much lying is going on at the expense of others? Is it an act of love to create an atmosphere so tense that employees are in a constant state of apprehension?

What about the schools or colleges in which we teach? Do we know if the education students are getting is useful to them as persons; is the financial burden too great for the education received? Are methods discussed, evaluated, improved? Actions, remedying similar situations, require a sincerity of purpose and are the outward expression of the fundamental belief that we are our brother's keeper.

On a global scale, only an all-encompassing effort on the part of many people will bring justice and peace. If each nation respects the other, thus moving in the right direction, then each will be able to "beat their swords into plowshares and their spears into pruning hooks. One nation shall not raise the sword against another, nor shall they train for war again" (Is. 2:4). Reports of sessions at the United Nations are evidence that many countries are committed to unselfish ideals. However, conflicts among member-nations caused by bigotries, prejudices, hatred are part of day to day proceedings of the General Assemblies of this organization dedicated to the removal of social ills and the implementation of human rights. We cannot hope to experience peace unless each person wishes it for others. This is true of us as individuals and as members in the family of nations.

We become spiritually aware of others when we come to understand ourselves. We find that we are not happy if we are locked continuously in an obsessive concern for self. This may call for a total renewal of self. Valid decisions depend on a basic understanding of the person, as a creature of God. Do we realize how dependent we all are on policy decisions made on the local, regional, national and international level? During the United Nations' Second Development Decade the goals are humane. Throughout the struggle for Human Rights, the whole person becomes important. Doesn't this give a Christian direction to the development of the world?

A significant little book published in Bombay in 1911 bears the title *Fortifying the Layman.*[3] The author shows the need for developing the contemplative as well as the acquisitive faculties of the Christian lay person. And Douglas Steer explains why this is important: "It is because man is a contemplative being that he cannot bear a condition of meaninglessness, of irresponsibility, without it rotting him out."[4] Our mission is to convert the modern world to the gospel, not to abolish it; to bring about a synthesis of gospel and the needs of *all* persons. Personal interest is to be sacrificed for the good of others. A spirit of love and understanding should permeate all deliberations. Persons, who are spiritually aware, find happiness and joy in life. They become "responsible participants in the whole of life, whether it be in school, in the factory, or in the office—or in any sector of the political, economic, and social worlds."[5] As a pilgrim people we go together to the Father and are in the process of becoming more fully His. The world in which we live is the same world which we help restore.

As Christians, therefore, we need to sort our thoughts with a competent spiritual director, if we are to grow in maturity of spirit. We need to have frequent dialogue, on a person-to-person basis with a skilled guide, a priest or minister perhaps, whose objective is the spiritual development of persons. The suggestion is that, having focused on the significance of decisions thus far, our present purpose in this chapter will be to explore the possibility of using the "Rules for the Discernment of Spirits" found in the *Spiritual Exercises* of St. Ignatius, as guidelines for decision-making in the public sector. Many priests and religious are accustomed to setting aside a period each year for the Spiritual Exercises; however, lay persons might well apply some of the principles contained in them to their daily experience.

It is necessary to repeat at the outset that prayer and penance are required because discernment means "to perceive or to recognize an inspiration of grace. . . Discernment at its deepest level supposes the habit of contemplation that cannot be acquired over a few weekends, intense as they may be. This principle applies as much to persons as to communities. It is of some importance that discernment should be made in a prayerful framework: it is of greater importance that those who discern should be prayerful persons."6 How can lay persons be prayerful? Do they have time for contemplation?

On a December morning in Carl Schurz Park, New York, it is possible to watch the sun rise, red and round. The new day slips into being. In its brightness windowpanes shine like jewels, buildings take on a rose cast; seagulls glide and swoop and dip toward the fast-moving currents of Hellgate, birds dart plucking berries off bushes, and squirrels hustle in dried leaves looking for a last kernel. We breathe—"Indeed, this is the day which the Lord has made. . . ." Locked in this beginning is potential. We chose to enjoy this moment of gladness. We could have ignored it completely, particularly, if preoccupied with the dread of another routine day. We decided one way, instead of the other, and in doing so changed ourselves for the better. We can find such moments of contemplation in the happenings of every day, even today, this morning. If deep-thinking penetrates our day, we will feel enriched and will meet others with grace and in peace, because Love is within close reach. If we develop "the habit of contemplation," our decisions will be spiritually significant.

For a moment let us consider present ways of deciding what we do. If we are in doubt about a certain course of action we use the simple test: "How do I feel about it? Do I feel awkward, uncomfortable, ill at ease, restless, if I am or were to be in a given situation? Common sense guides us toward positive and other-centered behavior, particularly if we remove the blinders of selfishness. When we act hastily, we discover sometimes that we acted unwisely by the reaction of another person, or the very consequences of our action tell us. We learn daily, though not always thoroughly, how to distinguish between good and bad behavior.

Then too, there is the gift of prudence, which we know as one of the gifts pf the Holy Spirit received at the time of Confirmation. Prudence is defined as "the right reason of things to be done"7 and consists in "the use of powers and habits"8 perhaps already existing within us. It presupposes a good disposition with regard to purpose and some moral virtue which rectifies the appetite. We should will to do right. This is essential to prudence, that we act out of right choice, not impulse or passion. If we are Christians who live by love, we are very apt to choose what is right. If we are prudent we realize the weight of our actions—that they affect our present lives and those of others and our forever-life. We act now and forever.

A right choice includes not only an end, but the means to that end. "Prudence is necessary to man that he may lead a good life, and not merely that he may become a good man."9 If we seek counsel of another, we should think about it carefully and prayerfully, and then make the choice our own as to how to be and what to do.

The discernment of good and evil influences is not an unnatural process. Let's think for a moment of how readily we discern body changes. We try to find quickly the source of any pain and decide on a remedy for it. (I have a tension headache, therefore I take aspirin and rest.) Usually, we are able to discern between a minor symptom and one which calls for the guidance of a professional.

When so many people are being or should be treated for depression, we cannot help wondering if there is not need for a better understanding of the movements of the soul, even to an elementary degree. If we have a problem or can't cope, more than likely, we choose *not* to think about it. How readily we turn to the medicine or liquor cabinets for the answer, and unwittingly become a part of the drug culture, as we seek distraction and relief in a drug, perhaps a tranquilizer, or alcohol. It is a staggering fact that in the book, *Drugs from A to Z: A Dictionary,*[10] the index totals 30 pages of drug names, 26 of which are with double columns. These are collected from reliable sources: Federal Bureau of Narcotics, the Journal of the American Pharmaceutical Association, Federal Bureau of Drug Abuse Control. The larger section is devoted to names of barbiturate, amphetamine and combination drugs. What does the abuse of these drugs say to us? Do we, or do we not, need a means of exploring the sources of negative thoughts and influences? Could the "Rules for the

Discernment of Spirits" be used to indicate how the Christian should deal with his thoughts in making decisions related to the ups and downs of daily living?

We have already mentioned that the demonic is present in this world and that the intent is to move us and our society away from God. Indeed, the spirit of evil diligently tries to disturb us by breeding thoughts of dissatisfaction, discouragement, despair and even pride. His quality of life is one of unrest and can easily be recognized. We are warned that: "There is a mystery of evil that exists not only in the consciousness and deliberation of man, but is found in every situation of human existence and is translated into those patterns of life that have worked to restrict, dominate and even destroy the human person."[11]

Students of art history and literature soon realize that one of the predominant themes of art-pieces or the classics is the contest that man has with the devil, evil forces, the enemy, Satan, the serpent, the dragon. If he is graced with success, he emerges a hero because his quest to conquer evil involved risk, dedication and continued endeavor. In recent times many were saying God is dead and at the same time denying the existence of the devil. More recently Jesus is alive on stage and screen, and satanic cults rise with the smoke of incense and patrons faint at the sight of possession in the movie, "The Exorcist." We have only to look within ourselves, really. We detect two opposing forces. And, haven't we ever looked at a friend and said, "She's impossible today, what's gotten into her?" God's heroes, the saints, are victorious over the evil which brings death to the soul, as Christ himself was victorious over death. It does no good to deny the existence of evil forces. Their power and evil practices pervade our streets and our homes and the chambers of government. It is essential to know how to deal with them. More important is it to know how to detect them.

At the same time we should be aware of our own inclination to evil, because of our fallen natures. During the ceremony of Baptism we renounce Satan and accept God as essential to our lives. Baptism gives faith, which is light because "it enables us to see in the darkness . . . to find our way, where without it we should be in danger of falling or losing ourselves."[12] With a determination on our part to move away from evil and to grow Christ-like buttressed by the strong support of a prayerful and sacramental life, we can aspire to the greatness of living Christ, which we are called to do as His own.

We have established, therefore, the need for rules for discernment in daily-life decisions affecting our own or other families, neighborhoods, cities, states, nations—and the world. In other words, Christians among us who participate in making important decisions in the public sector should apply these rules whenever possible. We will, therefore, devote the next two chapters to rules for individual and communal discernment. If they cannot be followed exactly in certain or all circumstances, at least they will serve as a guide and bring some enlightenment to the difficult but constant task of making Christian choices.

Chapter 6

RULES FOR INDIVIDUAL DISCERNMENT

Having already established the need for certain rules for discernment, in this chapter we shall try to examine closely two methods of discernment which would prove useful to Christian lay persons as they make decisions in their *personal* lives. In the following chapter we will consider rules for communal discernment, which will be useful to them in their work in the world. It will be noted that some characteristics are common to both individual and communal discernment.

To begin with let us remember that our feelings, memory, imagination, emotions, intelligence and will are involved in all our decisions. We should distinguish between the intellect and will, which are superior powers of the soul, and the "lower-memory": imagination, feelings (which are usually somewhat vague) and emotions (which are more definite such as joy or sadness, love or hatred, desire or despair). Spiritual writers tell us that *only* God can touch directly the upper, but He permits both good and evil spirits to affect the lower.[1] Thus intelligence and will can be directly and exclusively moved by God. In the simplest religious experience

We need to be aware of this distinction. Who, for example, was the mover of the following experience?

> . . . I was drawn back to Telgte on Easter Sunday. It was a crisp, windy day. Grayish white clouds, silhouetted against space, coasted about in curious and whimsical shapes. I had been there before, not very long ago . . . brought there by a friend. We lit a candle together and admired the air of expectancy and gratitude which framed little silver medallions shaped as hearts and crosses, manifesting favors prayed for and received. That day I didn't ask for a favor, but I was grateful that my friend had brought me there for a moment of peaceful sharing. I had told him I was tired of suffering and that I wished priests spoke more often of the Risen Christ.
>
> When I arrived in the chapel on Easter, I found I was alone. I slipped into the first bench and suddenly felt a rush of anxiety, a desire to make amends. The same brown wood-carved statue that had repulsed me momentarily on my first visit, because it reminded me of holding my dying infant and the crushing sensation that it was, this time brought thoughts of soothing exchange, of caress, reassurance.
>
> I remained very still and suddenly became aware of a person breathing . . . slow at first, then louder, then soft and regular again. I turned around to see if someone had joined me in the small chapel . . . I saw no one. I shook a little . . . wondering about this. As if wishing for company, I looked at the spot where my friend had stood, remembering what a special moment it had been. I imagined him there, but his image was faint, as if

enveloped in a mist or glow. Then, beyond an opening in the chapel wall, I was conscious of the back-side of a man's figure moving away. The outer garment was light tan, hair dark and somewhat long . . I was confused with wonder. I quickly left the chapel and went to the outer side of the semi-open wall, as if looking for a trace of him. I found only an indentation there in which were water and a place for candles. There was one candle burning, and yet no one seemed to be around.

Half-dismissing the incident as the work of my over-active imagination and still a little shaken, I walked to a nearby park and sat on a bench to eat some lunch. After a while I took a walk down a path lined on both sides by tall trees. It was at that moment that I felt an indescribable sense of wholeness, an integration of self and the Risen Christ. I felt that every step I took, He took with me. The sensation came quietly and went away as quietly. Before leaving Telgte I stopped once again where I had seen the water and the candle, and I blessed myself.

One day, almost a year later, when I had misgivings about the future, my thoughts returned to Telgte . . . I asked Jesus to interpret this experience for me . . . was I imagining things or did something really happen there? I had never really known what to make of it all. Since then things had not gone well; others made decisions which affected me deeply and which I found difficult to understand. If Jesus had consoled me at Telgte, he had asked still more of me!

He answered and seemed to speak of forgiveness, of love, of life, of the light that is His presence: "You may see my back, but my face is not to be seen" (Ex. 33:23). He seemed to assure me of the blessedness of true friendship, selfless kindness and concern, that we are not meant to travel "the way" alone, that he visits and speaks to us through others. He inspired me to follow the counsel of my friend. He seemed to say, 'The peace you felt is My peace, and is the same as eternal peace.'

"But how could I be sure that this interpretation was not my own invention or a delusion or deceit of the evil spirit? I believe it was His message because the same sense of peace, tranquility of spirit I knew at Telgte returned: faith, confidence and hope proclaimed once again with certainty that Jesus is our friend and speaks to us through others; accepting what He asks is our response . . . we go with Him and others towards the Father.

After reading through the following rules of discernment we will be in a better position to judge whether or not this was a sound evaluation.

This experience accentuates the necessity for and wisdom of remaining close to Christ through prayer and penance (and redemptive suffering). St. Ignatius, the contemplative "in the thick of the action," carefully built into his rules for discernment suggestions for both of these. In earlier chapters of this book we found prayer and penance in the foundation of the believing Christian's life: prayer in the Eucharistic liturgy, the highest form of prayer (St. Ignatius called it "the Center of all graces"[2]) and penance, in those sufferings we bring upon ourselves by sin and those we are obliged to endure in daily life. Why not, then, incorporate into our decision–making these elements, which give meaning to living already: *redemptive suffering transforming us into decisive workers by Christ's presence as celebrated in the Eucharist, with the vision of God's kingdom before us?*

The basic material for the subject of this chapter is the "Rules for Discernment of the Spirits," as included within the *Spiritual Exercises* of St. Ignatius and recommended for use during the first week.[3] (Each week is divided into exercises—for the well-being of the soul, as one would do bodily exercises. The exercises of the first week contain consideration and contemplation of sins.) *The Spiritual Journal of St. Ignatius Loyola* reflects, "the practical manner in which St. Ignatius adapted the essence of the *Exercises* to the concrete realities of life. He applies the principles and norms of the immortal little book, not in a time fixed and dedicated to a retreat and within the limits of the meditation made at such a time, but in the midst of the ordinary occupations of his life."[4] Father John Carroll Futrell, who has written extensively on this subject, says, "The goal of spiritual discernment is to find God and, therefore, to find His will—and not the other way around."[5] Later he states: "The goal of all spiritual discernment is the coinciding of one's own will with the universal will of God, as it is manifested and lived in the person of Jesus Christ."[6] In "Finding God's Will," Father Avery Dulles writes: "Man lives in a culturally pluralistic society, in which a bewildering number of world views and ethical systems compete for his allegiance. Social structures are in rapid flux; venerable precedent no longer holds unquestioned sway. Modern man is anxiously groping for a method and a logic which can help him find the course of action which is right for him as a particular person in a particular and rapidly changing situation. This need is felt with special urgency by earnest Christians in the spiritually momentous decisions of their lives. How can they be assured of finding the will of God?"[7] For the purpose of this book we might consider the following Rules as a useful and valuable instrument for more persons than presently use them by presenting them as gleaned from three written sources[8] and personal reflection.

(Source references found in note 8 will be referred hereafter by (I) St. Ignatius, (B) Burke, (D) Delmage.)

Rule 1. For those who move from mortal sin to mortal sin (which severs the bond of love between man and God), the enemy introduces thoughts of pleasures which will "plunge them deeper in their vice and sins" (I). The good spirit causes that same person to be conscious of sin and encourages remorse by introducing thoughts of loss, death and judgment. A check of our reactions on reading the daily newspaper gives us an idea of just how deep is our sensitivity to sin. If we reflect occasionally on what we would have done in a given situation we will further establish the degree of our personal proneness to good and evil.

Rule 2. Those who are striving to do good and be

better in the service of God will recognize that evil forces will cause anxiety and sadness, place obstacles in the way, and agitate with false reasoning so as to impede progress; the good spirit inspires them with courage and strength and even rewards them with consolation and peace, removing any blocks in the way of performing good works. The sincere and dedicated person often experiences seemingly unreasonable obstacles in the effort to accomplish an act of charity, sometimes in the person who is to be benefited. Consolation and peace come from God, reminding this person that this gesture of giving will mean something more to that person later by way of significance.

Rule 3. Spiritual Consolation. A consolation is an interior movement which raises us to exclaim "Praise Him." Our love of others is for God's sake. We weep for our sins. Or, our eyes are moist with joy when we see a good friend again, a newly ordained saying his first Mass, a young couple pledge their love, the smile of an infant, a sunrise, anything which speaks of His goodness and mercy. Our faith, hope and love grow. We lead others toward heavenly things naturally. We are "relaxed and at ease with the Lord" (D).

Rule 4. Spiritual Desolation. "The thoughts that spring from consolation are contrary to those that spring from desolation" (I). "Evil blankets the soul" (B). there is darkness and disquiet. We are attracted to pagan priorities, we are tempted and agitated, we are apathetic, we have no hope, nor love; we are sad, discouraged and quite depressed. This can be a very painful and debilitating state to be in and in current parlance we are literally "non-functioning," therefore, not only we, but those around us suffer. We drag them down with us into the mire of negativeness. We are separated from the Lord; we no longer see our role in the Paschal Mystery.

Rule 5. "In time of desolation we must never make a change, but remain firm and constant in the resolution and determination made on the day preceding this desolation, or in the preceding consolation." (I) This rule is worth while applying, for instance, in the case of job change. So often such a change is made without spiritual discernment, but with only practical matters considered.

Rule 6. In time of desolation we should not revise previous decisions, yet we should become more prayerful, meditate and examine our conscience, and do even the simplest penance that will curb the growth of depression. We might add to these a positive act of love toward another, such as writing a letter to someone who may need cheering or taking time to really listen to one of our children or our spouse. We should remember also that at such times we are difficult to live with and the sooner we bounce back to a comfortable level of living the happier all will be.

Rule 7. If God seems distant, if He does not

answer, if we seem apart from Him, disoriented, alone, it is because He has left us to our natural powers. Though He does not totally remove Himself from us, for we still have "grace sufficient for our eternal salvation" (I), he tests us so that we can resist temptation. We prove our love for Him by our faith in Him. The aloneness can go on for weeks and yet we know that He is with us. He is present *always*.

Rule 8. We should have courage in temptation. We should stir up hope, remembering that a new consolation is most likely to follow. This may not always be easy to do for some persons who have a tendency to despondency. Nature may provide just the relief needed to break the thrust of desolation for even if it is a gray day, we know the sun will shine again, or if it is dark, dawn will come. Certainly before finding a radical means of escape, we should try recommendations in rule 6.

Rule 9. If we are lazy about our spiritual life, if we pray at a minimum and even now think it unnecessary to attend Mass even on Sunday, we can expect to be cut off automatically, as it were, from spiritual consolation. Today, especially among young people, there seems to be a concern to serve others rather than to worship God on Sunday forgetting that it is the love and worship of God which activates the love for others and that it is not only possible, but necessary, to do both: to balance the contemplative and active parts of our lives. There is another reason for desolation which is "to help us find our own identity before God," by a realistic assessment of just how ready and how far we will put ourselves out for God *without consolation* (D). A third reason, is that desolation gives us a true knowledge of ourselves and our powerlessness in the face of God—all is a gift from Him, even His allowing desolation, so we need not have pride even by assuming that our own devotion made us weep.

Rule 10. While consoled we should think of a coming time of desolation and plan to meet it head on with all our energies primed to dispel depression. We are perhaps reminded here of the physical/emotional/intellectual cycles which we experience. Women particularly can prepare themselves for bouts of oncoming depression. However, when pressing family duties coincide with such times they are, in truth, called upon to meet demands "head on" and might, I suggest, make an expressed intention of redemptive suffering.

Rule 11. We should be humble in consolation, knowing that without God's grace and help we could not rise above desolation. And when we are caught in the mesh of desolation we should rely on God's strength and we will be given sufficient help to resist and overcome the enemy. It is well at such times to simply sit or lie perfectly still, or if near a church to enter it and sit quietly until some degree of peace returns. The intent is that we place ourselves completely in God's hands, knowing that without Him we cannot regain our joy and gladness.

Rule 12. The enemy should be met boldly with stout heart and he will have no real strength or power over us. We are apprehensive, however, and lose courage in resisting temptation, "there is no beast so fierce on the face of the earth as the enemy of our human nature in prosecuting with intense malice his wicked designs" (I), "for his whole desire in destroying us is to destroy mankind" (D). As we said in the previous chapter our own evil inclinations can prove to be our worst enemy and we must "be steadfast" in checking them. Selfishness can creep into our lives so easily, permeating them with a climate which robs them of all joy; for we find we are never satisfied.

Rule 13. The enemy prefers to conduct his business in secret, not in the open. The torment caused by soul-disturbance is quickly dispelled when shared with a spiritual counselor. However, often a person is held back by magnified inhibitions from seeking advice or a hearing, and it is God's grace which enables this venture toward relief. The role of healer which is primarily that of priest or minister (though lay persons are often called upon to listen) is an important one and can do much to reduce suicide statistics. If the enemy's words and suggestions are revealed to a priest in confession or during spiritual consultation, he knows that they lose their worth and his power over that person is diminished.

Rule 14. The enemy "studies our predominant

fault and works on that" (B). He seeks to possess us and therefore studies us well, finding out where we are strong and where we are weak. Each day we should try to do something to curb our predominant fault in order to discourage this sort of infiltration.

A second set of rules developed for the second week of *Spiritual Exercises* gives further help in the discernment process, because these exercises, largely in the form of contemplations, present solutions to possible confusion. We can often think something to be good which has only "the semblance of good."

Rule 1. "God and His angels generally excite true gladness and joy and remove sadness. The devil generally fights joy and spiritual consolation" and will do anything to disturb God-given peace and joy (B). "The mind is disturbed by sophistries masquerading as reasonable conclusions"(D).

Rule 2. God causes consolation *without* any preceding intermediate cause. The creator alone can go in and out of the soul moving it to conversion, an attraction to and total love of God. No object put before us, no act of our own understanding and will has produced it. God is present to us. This Presence of God within us can be keenly felt at times and should be moments for praise and glory.

Rule 3. When there in an immediate cause the consolation can be divine or diabolical in origin. Consolations from God lead to greater knowledge of good and better behavior. The demonic leads us toward moral failure and ruin. This rule is clear enough and is a good measuring stick, as it were. If a consolation inspires us to work better, to help another person, to love one's crotchety husband or wife more, then that consolation is from God and the instrument of that consolation is sent by God. How often do we consider ourselves as God's instruments of consolation to others? O happy thought!

Rule 4. The deceits of the devil are subtle. He encourages the spiritually aware in their holy and good thoughts, then he twists thinking with suspicions and behavior "into the hidden traps of his own irrational position" (D). Sensitive persons are often plagued by these deceits and need outside spiritual guidance to help them sift through the confusion, so as to retain the kernel of truth they were meant to retain and savor.

Rule 5. We should learn to watch the course of our thoughts: their origin, development and logical outcome. If in the beginning, middle and end our thinking leads to God, it is from God. If our thinking lures us away from good, or "incites us toward a lesser good than what we had previously sought or decided to do," we can be sure this is *not* divine guidance. "The same applies to whatever induces a sense of collapse, anxiety, or turmoil as a substitute for a previous state of well-being, serenity of outlook, and personal composure" (D). The evil spirit is the enemy of our advancement in the life of grace and love. Could it be that within a marriage when one partner is not following "divine guidance," this sense of collapse, anxiety and turmoil is visited upon the partner and that person is no longer able to function in a state of well-being and composure? In place of a life of grace and love, the marriage is bereft of what it was meant to have and becomes a "dead marriage." Haven't we seen examples of this repeated many times?

Rule 6. It is essential to review our good thoughts and to see where the enemy inserted himself into the picture; what good point he used to attract our attention. "Then we should judge how he tried little by little to pollute our previous enthusiasm for the religious aspect of that life situation and to contaminate our serenity of spirit" (D). In the future we can guard against his deceits. Motivations for doing a good act can be changed swiftly by a deceit of the enemy. God who inspires good works will suggest; then, the enemy will do everything to confuse so as to delay or prevent the good act from being performed . . . "of course you're doing it out of love, but aren't you forgetting your love of God—you shouln't love a person so much, and aren't you really doing it out of selfishness, so that you will benefit in turn; is that real charity?" Present-day emphasis on self-fulfillment, with its inherent dangers of excessive self-love and obsessive self-interest, indicate the need for careful attention to such variations in motivation.

Rule 7. While living the Paschal Mystery we experience various hints and cues for good or evil in our minds and hearts. Those with a good objective come softly, gently, "as a drop of water entering into a sponge" (I). Evil suggestions and impulses come in sharply, and with noise and disturbance, "like a drop of water falling on a rock" (I). For those with a deteriorating spiritual life, the influences are the opposite. An impulse contrary to that condition, therefore of good influence, is loud and sharp and upsets our deepest cravings, whereas if we are oriented toward evil, evil impulses "enter in silence, as into their own house, through the open doors" (I).

Rule 8. Consolation without any created cause is of divine origin, we have said, however, we must distinguish between the time of consolation itself and the time that follows immediately. During the latter we can assent to an idea and decide on an action which moves toward God or not. This may be due to the way we think usually and our former patterns of decision-making, or it may not be inspired immediately by God. "Therefore, ideas need competent evaluation before we give assent to them or carry them out into action" (D). It is well, therefore, to review briefly with a competent guide a decision made, thus confirming its validity.

A second method of discernment which should prove useful in making personal choices and which

was set down by St. Ignatius is as follows. He calls for
"a time of tranquility" when one considers

why I was born	to praise our Lord
	to save my soul
my choice	should help serve God
	save my soul
my disposition	indifferent—no inordinate affection
	I should be free to follow
	that which will give
	greater glory and praise
	to God and insure the
	salvation of my soul
prayer	that God will move my
	will to make the right
	choice and follow
	through on it
pros and cons	spiritual as well as
	practical advantages and
	disadvantages in relation
	to goal set above
make reasonable choice	"following weightier
	motions of reason"
	make decision, avoiding
	sensual motions
confirmation-prayer	offer decision to God and
	ask Him to confirm it—
	"if it be to His greater

service and praise"
assure Him that own will
is in tune with His

We can recognize that even with these two helpful aids to personal decision-making, we can make a choice which would seem later to have been a wrong one. It is then that we come in touch with the mystery of divine providence. Our lives become cluttered with difficulties and trials and we wonder, at times, if this is where we are to find our joy. Then, remembering that we are Christians, we place our trust in God, we choose the Christ-life, as it is, knowing that He will bring all to glory. As long as we try to live according to His loving guidance, we have the distinct consolation of experiencing in this life the peace of His Presence which we will have forever in the next.

Chapter 7

RULES FOR COMMUNAL DISCERNMENT

In the previous chapter we have explored, with some practical application, guidelines for personal or individual discernment. We should now give some consideration to the method suggested by St. Ignatius for communal discernment. Up to now this form of deliberation has been used mostly by persons in religious communities. It seems fair and useful to determine whether this method would be helpful to other groups as well.

Today organizations on all levels, with a wide variety of interests, have developed or used techniques for decision-making. Under terms such as group dynamics, consciousness raising, buzz groups, brainstorming sessions, they have arrived at some decision or consensus. In *Decision-Making Processes of the United Nations* consensus is defined as "a way of proceeding without formal objection." The document states that the General Assembly "is increasingly reaching decisions by means of consensus rather than by voting."[1]

It is interesting to note that in 1539, St. Ignatius and his companions arrived at a consensus in this way: "each person had his opportunity to speak, each was listened to respectfully, each man's arguments were welcomed and weighed. The striking contrasts will impress us: the freedom of spirit and docility to the Spirit, breadth of vision and allegiance to the Church, personal integrity and openness to others, astounding unity amid diversity of temperament and views. One can sense the warm esprit de corps: the mutual respect and affection, the sense of spiritual solidarity."[2] Is this so different from the quality of discussion sought today?

As William J. Byron, S.J., indicated to the Institute for Religious and Social Studies at the Jewish Theological Seminary of America in New York City the insights from the Jesuit experience can be adapted for use by other than religious groups. Even on such occasions it is necessary to test the spirits: " . . . do not trust every spirit, but put the spirits to a test to see if they belong to God . . . (1 Jn. 4:1). He emphasized qualities necessary in order to discern and decide well. One must be "(1) ready to move in any direction that God wants, therefore radically free; (2) open to sharing all that God has given him, therefore radically generous; (3) willing to suffer if God's will requires it, therefore radically humble (courageous); (4) questing for union with God in prayer, therefore radically spiritual."[3]

Any of us who has worked with groups has recognized a rhythm of uneasiness and peacefulness which literally dances throughout a discussion as both sides of an issue are aired, first one, then the other. The process of arriving at a consensus takes preparation, practice and precision. As Father Futrell points out before giving the steps in the Ignatian Method of Deliberation: "The deliberation itself begins, . . . only when all possible evidence has been gathered, clarified through discussion, and individually discerned, and when the active love of God in history has indicated through events that there is no more time for preparation, but a decision must be made now."4

The Steps in the Ignatian Method of Deliberation:

Prayer	1. Begin with prayer for light from the Holy Spirit, perhaps including an invitation to shared spontaneous prayer for a few moments. It might be well to 'situate' the prayer by readings from the Scriptures, the writings of the founder, or other documents expressing the spirit of the community.
Sharing Cons	2. Each person reports from his own individual discernment the reasons he has seen which militate against the proposed choice. These are recorded.

Prayer   3. At least a brief break. This must be long enough for each one prayerfully to reflect upon the results of step 2.

Sharing   4. Each person reports from his own
Pros   individual discernment the reasons he has seen which favor the proposed choice. These are recorded. At the end of this step, find out whether it is already immediately clear to everyone from the recorded con and pro reasons what the election should be. If so, go immediately to step 7. If not, proceed to step 5.

Prayer   5. A break period for each one prayerfully to reflect upon the results of step 4 in the light of those of step 2.

Evaluation 6. The effort is made now to evaluate
and   the weight of the reasons con and
Discovery   pro recorded and then, in the light of this evidence, communally to discern the choice to which the community is called by God. If the Holy Spirit is working through the

second time of election, and if the conditions of authentic communal discernment has been fulfilled, the decision finally should be clear, and confirmation should be experienced unanimously through shared deep peace—finding God together.

Prayer 7. The deliberation session should end with a prayer of thanksgiving and of offering the election to the Father with a reaffirmation of corporate commitment to carry out the decision. Perhaps this could include an invitation to spontaneous shared prayer.[5]

Communal discernment as used in making decisions requires a certain maturity. Interpersonal dialogue implies a spirit of give and take with no one dominating the conversation. This is true of any exchange between members of any group. Above all, it is very necessary that the lines of communication remain open and that persons be really present to one another. It is important to allow time to reflect on one another's thoughts. Within a group it is essential that each one participate in presenting various viewpoints, diverse opinions. It is in this diversity that there can be any hope of unity and a consensus reached. If the majority agree, others should register their reasons for abstention. This procedure is always in effect at the United Nations where diversity is the constant climate. To quote from same source, "In using consensus, the rights of the minority to express their reservations must be protected and consensus should not be interpreted as unanimity."[6] One might ask if it is possible, in a gathering of such varied cultures and persuasions and political pulls, to ever hope for unanimity. Yet, it seems, the effort to do so is well spent.

If a group is attempting to make a decision, and there are two irreconcilable forces, because some individuals are tightly closed and will not be open to the opinions of others, it could be that another among those present can break the stalemate by asking a question for clarification. This technique seems to relieve tension and gives the hard-bound a chance to listen with the possibility of enlightenment. The discussion for the purpose of decision-making will continue most likely in a productive fashion. Or as one author cautions: " . . . if someone is hampered by intellectual prejudice, ultimately he can be saved only by himself although the community that surrounds him can be an instrument of grace."[7]

Further very helpful guidelines have been developed by other authors which will assist in avoiding pitfalls usually encountered in both personal and communal discernment.[8] Of particular interest are

Psychological Notes on the Spiritual Exercises by W. W. Meissner, S.J.[9] These also include further notes on the discernment of spirits.

When working in groups which are multi-national or inter-faith or ecumenical and the formula for discernment is not used, it is possible, it seems, for one or several members to interject the desire that God's will be of first consideration. Even if there is no instance of general prayer, a few persons or even one of those present, can offer privately a prayer that all will be open to His inspiration. These few should have trust that God will lead the participants to the right goals. The desire to respond to His grace guarantees our nearness to Him. Sometimes one of a group, who may not be especially gifted, will surprise all participants by making, suddenly and quietly, a statement with the weight of gold. Divine insight comes to anyone who is open to it, particularly if it comes from a realization that we need God's help in all of our decisions. We read that "Nothing is more characteristic of Ignatius than (his) spiritual liberty, this total openness to the will of God manifested in the workings of divine providence in daily life."[10] Certainly it is evident throughout history that negative forces affect the lives of countless thousands. If we wish to be instruments of peace-making and peace-keeping, then careful decision-making is to be more valued than ever and we should develop a sharp eye for the divine and the diabolical in the events of universal history: the unrest stirred by the evil one and the peace which comes from God. One author goes so far as to say that "the ineffectiveness of modern Christianity is its failure to take evil seriously and deal directly with it."[11] We should help one another see both sides of life: sin and glory. On the natural plane alone: "There is growing recognition that the earth and its resources are finite and the peoples and nations of the world are interdependent and will survive or perish together."[12] On a global scale there is expressed need for priorities, for coordination, for cooperation and planned strategy, long and short range goal-setting, and, most of all, implementation. The implementation phase is the one which demands the serious dedication of all people. Indeed, it requires the sense of responsibility and discipline inspired by the gospels.

We should live each day of our marriage between the natural and supernatural with faith, knowing that the immanent and transcendent God is immensely concerned with our affairs and what we do about them. We know too that without Him we can do nothing, and are only too prone to seek selfish ends. If we become absorbed in "divinizing" His world, however, we become absorbed in the possibility of a future with Him. Our hope in Him, present today and magnificently promised, are joined.

It was Pierre Teilhard de Chardin who synthesized between the two faiths: "in what lies ahead of us and the faith in what lies above us, that is to say, faith in the two faces of the indissolubly immanent and transcendent God."[13] The synthesis of these two was his essential vocation. It is the vocation of every Christian as well. The world will lose its way unless guided and sustained by the people of God: "With the help of the Holy Spirit it is the task of *the entire people of God*, especially pastors and theologians, to hear, distinguish, and interpret the many voices of our age, and to judge them in the light of the divine Word. In this way, revealed truth can always be more deeply penetrated, better understood, and set forth to greater advantage."[14] Church and World co-exist in service to one another. The participants attending the Conference on Decision-Making at the United Nations expressed this concern: "we must build the spirit and dedication of the members in order to breathe life into the decision-making process. Without such increased will, the best decision-making procedures will result in an efficient but useless machine."[15] Or as Paul has written: "Do not conform yourselves to this age but be transformed by the renewal of your mind, so that you may judge what is God's will, what is good, pleasing and perfect" (Rom. 12:2).

Chapter 8

FAITH AND GLORY

This chapter will bring together our faith-hope-love commitment and the fulfillment that resides in it. It can be said that we know and love glory even now, as we move toward final transformation in Christ. Indeed, "the duty of man is to recognize and praise the divine glory."[1] It is not only our duty, but our chief end: "I will give thanks to you, O Lord, my God . . . and I will glorify your name forever" chants the psalm (86:21). When He rescues us we should be "loud in his praise" (Lk. 4:15), or as Karl Rahner phrases it: "There must be talk of God in order to give him glory."[2] Our praise can be transmitted to others: "You have been purchased, and at a price. So glorify God in your body" (1 Cor. 6:20). His act of love unites all of us in such a way that the power and glory that is Christ, transforms us into persons who share that power and glory. Praise Him!

If we think carefully we may remember and be able to tell about "moments of glory" in our lives, experiences which have an other-worldly quality; He is so near that we are fully conscious of His presence. His touch of glory may be slight, but profound. His power energizes us for the present life and tells us of what is to come. A time of glory is a time of conversion and renewal.

For some, an assembly of people gathered to share their spiritual insights for the purpose of healing serve as occasions for revelation. The impact of such moments can be tremendous; "Divine love may give itself with such overwhelming power that man perceives nothing but the crushing majesty of the Glory, and his response is concentrated into a single answer, utter obedience . . . ," a "graced response," without question.3 Persons, as a result, call themselves "charismatics"—as one explained: "I feel moved to go to Florida. I know there is some work for me to do there." Authors familiar with the development of this dimension in the life of the contemporary Christian trace the movement's progress, its pros and cons; for here again there is need for evaluation and discernment.4

In our daily lives Jesus heals and transforms continually in many different ways. At times, we find He infuses into our minds, without any feverish effort on our part, clear and penetrating thoughts. Paul prayed for his fellow Christians: "May the God of our Lord Jesus Christ, the Father of glory, grant you a spirit of wisdom and insight to know him clearly" (Eph. 1:17). The man Jesus who revealed Himself as the divine Son of God the Father by restoring the sick to health, and raising the dead to life, is today that same healer, the giver of life. If we are spiritually aware, we watch for these enlightenments; for indeed, they are the Risen Jesus in all His glory speaking to us, lifting us from the morass of doubt and uncertainty to the level of living which began with visible healings recorded in the gospels.

His healing comes to us through events, such as the actual meeting and being with people who reinforce by their very presence all that we believe in and hope for. When moved to recognition by grace, we see the Risen Christ in them and are enriched by these encounters. It is the eyes of faith that enable us to perceive His spirit within them. They communicate His glory by what they say and how they say it; in the soft, gentle tone of the Spirit. The ready heart which responds to an overture of Christ-love assures a continuity between faith and glory (I believe in you and love you . . . oh, the glory of it!).

Without a word spoken to us some faces manifest glory lodged deeply in the eyes. The sick, for example, who wait for deliverance may already know His glory and wait in peace for fulfillment. In Chapter 3 we examined thoroughly the creativity in transfigured suffering and how it speaks to us of God. We saw that it was Jesus' obedience to the will of the Father that made His apparent failure a success: "This Son is the reflection of the Father's glory" (Heb. 1:3). He asked us to be spared, but only if the Father so willed. This was not a passive acceptance, but a grasping of the cross, a total giving; love despite apparent desertion. At a parish discussion one person cited difficulty with the "distance" between Jesus and us because of His divinity. Might we not say that if we choose to accept His grace, and say our "fiat," there will no longer be distance, but blessed nearness?

Where else can we find His glory in our immediate lives? In nature's performances: the rising and setting of the sun. We see it in the first forsythia, the shapes of flowers (at Easter like trumpets and horns heralding the Risen One), the diversity among animals, the waters and all they contain, a breeze, a shell, a child. St. Ignatius used the actual and concrete world around him to emphasize spiritual joy. In the fourth week of the *Spiritual Exercises*, he recommends: "to avail myself of light, the beauties of the season, as in spring and summer of refreshing coolness, and in winter of the sun or of a fire in proportion as the soul thinks or conjectures that they can help it to rejoice in its Creator and Lord."5

Innumerable scripture passages present everyday images and symbols which help us to understand His glory: "Like the bow which appears in the clouds on a rainy day was the splendor that surrounded him. Such was the vision of the likeness of the glory of the Lord" (Ez. 1:28). When our Lord was transformed before Peter, James and John, a voice came from a cloud and said "This is my Son, my Chosen One. Listen to him!" (Lk. 9:35). The appearances of the

Risen Christ to his disciples are simply told, but weigh heavy with significance; a foreshadowing of our own glorification as recounted so enthusiastically by Paul: "Just as we resemble the man from earth, so shall we bear the likeness of the man from heaven (1 Cor. 15:49). "Splendor," "majesty," *"lumen gloriae"*; his glory lights up the pages of the Bible with dramatic visual accounts for our benefit and instruction.

God shows His glory through the lives of the saints, which follow one another down through history, manifesting his close contact with His chosen ones. He inspired them to write documents rich with spiritual significance. He speaks with them, giving them glimpses of His glory, which help to sustain them as they proceed toward fulfillment and complete union with Him.

God's glory is manifest in the Church which moves towards becoming a world-wide communion of faith and love, dynamically alive with God's eschatologically victorious grace in Christ. Despite apparent back-sliding due to human weakness, it leads the world invincibly towards the perfection of God's kingdom. The ordained members of the Church frequently show glory as they "knowingly, freely, gratefully accept what God has achieved perfectly through Christ, and manifest it in their whole lives."6

Our own work in the world is transformed by God's activity in us as He brings His kingdom to full glory. Efforts to bring about reconciliation between the family members are not without radiance. The development of the mind through education, the care of the body through careful nutrition and exercise reveal what is good. The development of the spirit according to the gospel spoken by God's ministers; liturgical events in even the smallest community praise His glory. The quiet prayer of sexual dedication between husband and wife, the search for evaluation by theologians, the act of charity (yes, even the homemade toy!) all that is good, true and beautiful is of God.

Our understanding of God's Fatherhood is very basic to the development of trust and resulting security, necessary for the full emergence of the human person. "See what love the Father has bestowed on us in letting us be called children of God!" (1 Jn. 3:1). Should we not shout with joy when we begin to realize what this means? If we have faith, it means we can say "God is love" in the midst of successive frustration; it means we can say "God is good" at "the utmost point of disgust with life."7 If we have faith we can rise again after numerous disappointments. If we have faith, we know courage and patience despite our fallen natures. Sometimes everything we are must go into an act of faith, especially when it does not come easily. We may be weak and tremble with the effort, even resist the grace. However, we know that God, the Father, who understands that we are tired and beaten, rescues us and enables us to rededicate ourselves to His purposes. Our faith then is made stronger and capable of conditioning us for whatever will happen to us in the future.

How many lives are predictable really? And yet, we know that we do not need to spend one moment wondering what life is all about. God is our destiny. His will, that we live forever with Him in glory, is the stimulus and purpose built into our lives by our faith commitment, made at Baptism. What happens to us is largely a result of choices for "God is not a projection which we slowly come to understand as such, but we ourselves are God's projection, set up in autonomy and freedom."[8] With our God-given freedom we choose how we will react to the persons and events we meet. We do not live for ourselves, but for others and for those who will come after us. We pass on to others the condition of humanity as we leave it. We cannot turn back. We cannot retouch or redo. How often do we realize that what we are and do today, lasts and is passed on to future generations? During our short span of years on this earth, we cannot hope to take significant strides, but we can continue the good that others have started and which will be continued by those who follow us. The eschatological dimension in our lives makes us realize the transient quality of our actions and at the same time their permanence. We act in time for eternity, knowing that what we do will not last, but the effect will last forever. Our efforts are but one step on the pilgrimage to completion.

Perhaps, then, we see why it is important that we make correct decisions which are arrived at within a climate of prayer, openness and humility, with a readiness to receive divine insight in an atmosphere of renewal and reconciliation. How different this is from the hasty judgment made while in an irritable mood caused by minor ills or vices, or the one made under pressure after a Martini lunch! Individual and group decisions affect all of us, some profoundly affect us. If the choice is a good one and acted upon with the right intention, even a routine task, resulting from that choice, is transformed into a means of perfection or personal fulfillment because it manifests God's glory.

We realize now that our challenge is not in the amphitheater, as it was for early Christians, but rather is a testing by forces and inclinations to evil which distort, confuse and create anxiety, tension, and depression within us. We are tossed in every direction on media waves which often threaten to submerge us into passivity. Overexposed to values which are incompatible with our own, we experience conflict within ourselves. Sometimes, in matters of great question, for example the life sciences, we are close to playing God. While exploring and discovering, are we meant to be able to answer *all* the questions and if we could, would there be room for faith? It is the inexplicable that nurtures faith. We are meant to explore, to discover, to initiate, to create.

Therefore, we understand that as Christians we have an obligation to discern carefully each movement of the soul. We know that if we accept even the slightest inconvenience in loving union with Jesus, we have fertile ground for the development of the discernment process. If we receive Christ in the Eucharist, we know that the call to faith is a call to risk and sacrifice, but not without a touch of glory.

We realize that we live with human frailty on the part of ourselves and others, and so look for alternatives when confronting an impasse. Just as a lively stream of water, when blocked, seeks another way to achieve its goal, so too our lives can become even more productive, because of deeply-felt initiatives. Our enthusiasm stamps out apathy and despair. We act decisively, knowing that at times we will have difficulties despite confirmation of decision. If we try and things go differently than expected, we can continue to be creative—not overcome, nor in disarray—but rather, hopeful, watching for signs of other ways to fulfill God's commands, "assisting the birth of hope" where it exists.

If it can be said that God hopes—He hopes that we will not be able to live without Him and that in time of adversity and discovery, we cannot relinquish our hold on Him, because to whom else can we turn? In our knowing and unknowing, we come to find God, we come to rely on Him, we move ever closer in that union He longs to have with us. In speaking of the individual Christian: "God must remain God for him, the God who is greater than all (than all the things he discovers) and nearer than all (than all the things which press upon him)."9

Faith and glory are continually and closely linked throughout the history of our own lives pulsating with promise: "So long as man remains on earth. he must be content to walk by faith, reverently inclining his mind and will before the word of God. At the end of time faith will issue into vision, and the revelation will be clearly perceived by the help of the light of glory."10

The eschaton is full glory manifest forever. This promise which is already hinted at on earth is the foundation of the Christian life. The glimpse of what is hoped for gives the Christian a perspective with unlimited possibility. Sheer faith is transformed into peace, joy and love which come from God. We are alive and in His favor. We experience a tangible intensity which confirms the personal presence of God. Throughout our lives, we can reach and touch the hand of Him who made us, who loves us and waits for our particular day of completion.

The glory of God is about us in our sadness and our joy. When darkness enfolds us, we need have no fear that He will abandon us; He enables us to remember those moments of glory in our lives or the lives of others, so that we may continue to be sure and secure in His love. Having "seen" the transfigured Christ, we can then come down form the mountain to do His work, by being "a distinctively Christian presence in the world."11

God's people should rejoice and are glad, for "in the midst of struggle they can see in faith the heavenly Jerusalem, while waiting for it to reveal itself fully to them."12

> Who is this King of glory!
> The Lord, strong and mighty,
> The Lord, mighty in battle . . .
>
> Who is this King of glory?
> The Lord of hosts;
> he is the King of glory.
>
> (Ps. 24:8,10)

MAY THE WHOLE WORLD BE FILLED WITH HIS GLORY (Ps. 72:19).

Appendix

SUGGESTED EXAMEN OF ATTITUDES

1. What is my attitude toward God? Do I understand that He created me out of love? Am I grateful for the confidence He has placed in me? Do I use my skills for the good of others? How can I serve God better realizing the purpose He has for me in this world?

2. What is my attitude toward religious practice? Do I rather not attend services because I don't get anything out of them? Do I consider the fact that their value for me depends on my disposition? Do I realize the necessity of maintaining close contact with God through prayer? What can I do to set an example of loyalty to God and Church?

3. What is my attitude toward my minister or pastor? If negative, why? How can I get him to accept my co-operation instead of anticipating criticism? Taking into account my particular training or talent how can I help him share his many responsibilities?

4. What is my attitude toward other church members? If their views are different from mine do I withhold my friendship? Do I insult them by telling them they are all wrong? Couldn't we both learn from an exchange of ideas?

5. What is my attitude toward my family? Do I believe my parents aren't "with it?" Could I be more open with them? How can I as a parent help my children live in this era of rapid change? Do I consider my home and family as more important to society than some would think and give them the necessary time and energy?

6. What is my attitude toward my neighbors on the street, bus or at work? If they are of a different creed or color do I rather not associate with them? Do I realize that they have problems also? Is there something I could do to make them feel accepted and loved?

7. What is my attitude toward my employer? Do I give him a full day's work for my pay? If I think changes should be made do I use peaceful means to bring them to light? Do I recognize that high-level job responsibility is demanding which may explain apparent neglect on the part of my boss?
8. What is my attitude toward community needs? Do I leave it all to the other person? Am I apathetic when asked to head a committee? What can I do to eliminate the deterioration of low-income families or the neglect of the children of the solvent?
9. What is my attitude toward society in general (state, nation, world)? Have I failed to express the Christian ethic at a time when such witness was needed? How can I spread Christ's message to others at my plant, in the hospital or office where I work? How often do I follow trends without discernment, forgetting that my actions are an expression of faith? Am I a responsible voter?
10. What is my attitude toward myself? Do I value the life that is in me as a gift of God to be cared for through sensible means? Am I open and joyous or do I let myself prefer to wallow in self-pity or discouragement? Do I understand that it is in doing for others that I find happiness? Do I use discernment when making personal choices? Do I see my life as one of continual spiritual growth and try to cooperate with God's action within me?

A CHRISTIAN'S PRAYER

O Lord Jesus, you came on earth to teach me how to live by the spirit. I love the challenge you have set before me.

If my heart and mind are open I will find myself surrounded, even caught up in your presence. Give me the grace to do what is necessary to remain in it and to understand why it is your wish to possess me.

Let me shout of your kindness. Help me to share your love-life with others in a ready and hopeful way.

In my own sphere of influence help me to bring the joy of presence and promise which you blend so beautifully as you live among us.

It is in you that I will find the nourishment which will strengthen my faith and help me to continue your work in the world. Guide me to those who will not live, unless I lead them to you.

Show me how to communicate with others so that we shall make choices in fidelity to your design and plan. It is through my co-operation and that of all your people that all things will be restored to you.

Help me to realize the importance of each moment of my life, its trials and joys. It is through them that I accomplish your work. Help me to understand this trust you have in me.

Touch me with your glory, so I shall know what to expect in your kingdom. Give me the grace to hope until I am united with you in eternity.

INTRODUCTION

1. As quoted in "As Others See Us," Anthony Lewis. *New York Times*, March 17, 1973.

2. Rev. William Thompson, S.S., "Rahner's Theology of Pluralism," appearing in "The Ecumenist," Jan-Feb. 1973.

3. As quoted in *Teilhard de Chardin Album,* Jeanne Mortier and Marie-Louise Auboux. (New York: Harper and Row, 1966), p. 63.

4. *Ibid.,* p. 64.

Chapter 1—OUR DYNAMIC SIGNIFICANCE

1. Hans Urs von Balthasar, "The Gospel as Norm and Test of all Spirituality in the Church," *Concilium,* 9, (New York: Paulist Press, 1966), p. 17.

2. Avery Dulles, S.J., *The Survival of Dogma.* cf. Chapter 7, "The Magisterium in a Time of Change," pp. 108-124.

3. *Tomorrow Began Today,* Education Seminar for Superiors General, "Religious Congregations at the Service of Today's Educational World." Rome, 1970.

4. Ferdinand Klostermann, "The Laity," *Commentary on Documents of Vatican II,* Chapter 4. (New York: Herder and Herder, 1968), p. 236.

5. Dulles, *op. cit.*, p. 116.

6. "The Theology of Earthly Realities and Lay Spiritu-ality." *Concilium*, 19, (New York: Paulist Press, 1966), p. 58. Cf. also, *Faith: Can man still believe?* in which Louis Monden, S.J., sees a period of "lay theology" now dawning. Tr. Joseph Donceel, S.J. (New York: Sheed and Ward, 1969), p. 205.

7. Yves Congar, O.P., *Lay People in the Church*. Tr. Donald Attwater. (Westminster, Md., Newman Press, 1957), p. 407.

8. (New York: Alba House, 1972).

9. This is particularly true of delegates and representatives of non-governmental organizations at the United Nations where an inter-disciplinary approach is desired in solving the problems which face the peoples of the world.

10. United Nations document (E/CN4/1028/Add. 4), 26 February, 1970.

11. Edith Hamilton, *The Greek Way to Western Civilization*. (New York: Mentor Books, 1962), p. 242.

12. *Listening to Lay People*, compiled by Cameron P. Hall. (New York: Friendship Press, 1971), p. 15:

13. Charles Baumgartner, *"Formes Diverses de l'Apostolat,"* *Christus* No. 13, (1957), pp. 9-33.

14. M. C. D'Arcy S.J., *The Pain of This World and the Providence of God.* (New York: Longmans, Green & Co., 1935), p. 129

15. Pierre Teilhard de Chardin. (New York: Harper & Row, 1972–Perennial Library ed.), pp. 49, 50

Chapter 2—MINISTRIES OF FAMILY LIFE

1. Address on receiving Honorary Doctorate at Catholic University of America, Washington, D.C. (United Nations Press Release SG/SM/1993-13 May 1974).

2. Enid Nemy, "Bewildered Husbands Seek Family Therapy." *New York Times*, Oct. 16, 1974.

3. Yves Congar, O.P., *Lay People in the Church*. Tr. Donald Attwater. (Westminster, Md., Newman, 1967), p. 202.

4. W. W. Meissner, S.J., M.D., "Notes on the Psychology of Hope," *Journal of Religion and Health* 12 (1973), p. 133.

5. *Believing*. (New York: Doubleday, 1974), p. 41.

6. Rosemary Goldie, Undersecretary of Vatican Council for the Laity and member of Vatican Special Standing Committee on Role of Women in Society, as quoted in *St. Louis Review*, August 2, 1974.

7. Reported in statement given by Paul Coste, Chief, UNESCO Section of Educational Structures, Dept. of Curriculum, Methods and Structures at UNICEF Executive Board Session, 13-24 May 1974, New York.

8. Dr. Nina Lief. This Center is a joint project of the New York Junior League and New York Medical College and is housed in the basement of Holy Trinity (Episcopal) Church.

9. W. W. Meissner, S.J., M.D., *Journal of Religion and Health*, 13 (1974), p. 39.

10. Paul Coste.

11. *Ibid.*

12. Nels F.S. Ferré, *Strengthening the Spiritual Life.* (New York: Harper, 1951), p. 63.

13. *Open to the World.* Tr. Dennis Doherty, O.S.B. and Carmel Callaghan (Baltimore: Helicon, 1966), p. 81.

Chapter 3—REDEMPTIVE SUFFERING

1. As quoted in *A History of Apologetics*, Avery Dulles. (New York: Corpus, 1971), p. 109.

2. Ida Friederike Görres, *The Hidden Face.* (London· Burns and Oates, 1959), p. 279. A study of St. Thérèse of Lisieux.

3. Barnabas M. Ahern, *Men of Prayer, Men of Action: Christian Spirituality Today.* (New York: Bruce, 1971), p. 91.

4. *Markings.* (New York: Alfred A. Knopf, 1964), p. 104.

5. (New York: Harcourt Brace Jovanovich, 1973), p. 212.

6. (London: Burns & Oates, 1958), p. 90.

7. United Nations document A/8844, 19 Oct. 1972.

8. *The Text of The Spiritual Exercises of Saint Ignatius*, tr. from original Spanish. (London: Burns and Oates, 1908), p. 106.

9. For an impressive development of "diminishment" see pp. 80 to 94 of *Le Milieu Divin* (London: Collins-Fontana Books, 1960).

10. Joseph Blenkinsopp, "We Rejoice in Our Sufferings," in *The Mystery of Suffering and Death*, ed. Michael J. Taylor, S.J. (New York: Alba House, 1973), p. 53.

11. Jürgen Moltmann, "Resurrection as Hope." *Ibid.*, p. 176.

12. (New York: Doubleday, 1971), p. 70.

13. As reported in *St. Louis Review*, June 20, 1974. Words of Msgr. Tibor Meszaros, secretary to Cardinal Mindszenty.

14. This information obtained from Rev. Avery Dulles, S.J.

Chapter 4—SHARING THE JOY OF CHRIST'S PRESENCE

1. *Le Milieu Divin*. (London: Collins Fontana Books, 1957), p. 82.

2. Yves Raguin, S.J. "Chastity and Friendship," *The Way*, Supplement 19, Summer, 1973, p. 111.

3. Ignace Lepp, *The Ways of Friendship*. (New York: Macmillan, 1966), p. 23.

4. Betrand Weaver, C.P., *Joy*. (New York: Doubleday-Image, 1964), p. 18.

5. *Love and Will*. (New York: W. W. Norton & Co., Inc., 1969), p. 289.

6. List adapted from one created by Neurotics Anonymous

International Liaison, Inc. 1967 as it appeared in the *New York Times*, 1973.

7. Jeanne Mortier and Marie-Louise Aboux, *Teilhard de Chardin Album*. (New York: Harper and Row, Pub., 1966), p. 193.

8. Chapter 5, "Places: The New Nomads" in *Future Shock* by Alvin Toffler will give thoughts on the subject of mobility.

9. Avery Dulles, S.J., "Faith Come of Age," *America*, 124 (1967), p. 137.

10. The "Universal Declaration of Human Rights" adopted and proclaimed by the United Nations 25 years ago on December 10, 1948 deserves our careful consideration.

11. Francis K. Drolet, S.J., *New Communities for Christians*. (New York: Alba House, 1972), p. 68.

12. *Ibid.*, p. 44.

13. Johannes B. Metz, *Theology of the World*. (New York: Herder and Herder, 1969), p. 119.

14. Karl Rahner, S.J., *Encounters With Silence*. Tr. James M. Demske, S.J. (Westminster, Md., The Newman Press, 1964), p. 56.

15. P. Benoit, O.P., *The Eucharist in the New Testament*. A Symposium, Tr. E. M. Steward, (Baltimore, Helicon Press, 1964), p. 86.

16. Hugo Rahner, Saint Ignatius Loyola—*Letters to Women.* (New York, Herder and Herder, 1960)..

Chapter 5—WHO AND WHAT INFLUENCES OUR DECISIONS?

1. (New York: Doubleday Image, 1971).

2. John Carroll Futrell, S.J., *Making An Apostolic Community of Love*, (St. Louis: The Institute of Jesuit Sources, 1970), pp. 231, 185.

3. Ernest R. Hull, S.J.

4. *Work and Contemplation.* (New York: Harper and Brothers, 1957), p. 21.

5. Quoist, *op. cit.* p. 64.

6. Ladislas Orsy, S.J., "Toward A Theological Evaluation of Communal Discernment," *Studies in the Spirituality of Jesuits*, V (1973), pp. 157, 178.

7. *Basic Writings of Saint Thomas Aquinas*, Anton C. Pegis, Ed. (New York: Random House, 1944), p. 435.

8. *Ibid.*, p. 435.

9. *Ibid.*, p. 437.

10. Richard R. Lingeman. (New York: McGraw-Hill, 1969), pp. 248-277.

11. Bernard Cooke, S.J. "Existential Pertinence of Religion," *Concilium*, 19 (New York: Paulist Press, 1966), p. 41.

12. A.–M. Roguet, O.P., *Christs Acts Through Sacraments.* (Collegeville, Minn.: The Liturgical Press, 1953), p. 60.

Chapter 6—RULES FOR INDIVIDUAL DISCERNMENT

1. Thomas A. Burke, S.J., "Rules For The Discernment of Spirits," A Brief Commentary. (Jersey City, N.J. 07302, Program to Adapt the Spiritual Exercises, 144 Grand Street), p. 1.

2. *The Spiritual Journal of St. Ignatius Loyola*, Feb. 1544-45. Tr. William J. Young, S.J. Orig. pub. Woodstock College Press 1958. Reprint by Program to Adapt the Spiritual Exercises 1971.

3. We will also consider the rules for the second week.

4. *The Spiritual Journal of St. Ignatius Loyala, Ibid., v.*

5. John Carroll Futrell, S.J., "Communal Discernment: Reflections on Experience," *Studies in the Spirituality of Jesuits* (St. Louis, Mo., The Institute of Jesuit Sources) IV (1972), p. 162.

6. *Ibid.*, p. 164.

7. *Woodstock Letters* (Spring, 1965). Reprint available from Program to Promote the Spiritual Exercises, p. 140.

8. *The Text of the Spiritual Exercises of St. Ignatius.* Tr. from Original Spanish. (London: Burns and Oates, Ltd., 1908). *Spiritual Exercises of St. Ignatius Loyola,* Lewis Delmage, S.J. (New York: Joseph F. Wagner, Inc., 1968). "Rules For The Discernment of Spirits," Thomas A. Burke, S.J. as cited above. Another translation available: *The Spiritual Exercises of St. Ignatius.* Tr. Anthony Mottola, Ph.D. with introduction by Robert W. Gleason, S.J. (New York: Doubleday-Image, 1964).

Chapter 7–RULES FOR COMMUNAL DISCERNMENT

1. Ninth conference on the United Nations of the Next Decade, Vail, Colorado, June 9-16, 1974, sponsored by The Stanley Foundation, p. 11.

2. Dominic W. Maruca, S.J., "The Deliberation of Our First Fathers," *Woodstock Letters* (July 1966). Reprint from Program to Promote the Spiritual Exercises, p. 326.

3. "Group Decision Making–Insights from the Jesuit Experience," January 18, 1972. *Catholic Mind*, 71 (1973), pp. 27-34.

4. Futrell, "Communal Discernment: Reflections on Experience," *Ibid.*, pp. 172, 173.

5. *Ibid.*

6. The Stanley Foundation, *op. cit.*, p. 12.

7. Orsy, *op. cit.*, p. 157.

8. These are available through the Program to Promote the Spiritual Exercises or The Institute of Jesuit Sources, Fusz Memorial, 3700 West Pine Blvd., St. Louis, Mo. 63108.

9. *Woodstock Letters*, 92 (1963) 349-366; 93 (1964), 31-58 and 165-191.

10. Futrell, *Making An Apostolic Community of Love*, p. 125.

11. Morton T. Kelsey, "The Mythology of Evil," *Journal of Religion and Health*, 13 (1974), p. 17.

12. The Stanley Foundation, *op. cit.*, p. 3.

13. Claude Cuénot, "Teilhard and The Spiritual Exercises of Saint Ignatius," reprint from *The Teilhard Review*, Winter 1969/70, Program to Adapt the Spiritual Exercises, p. 51.

14. *Gaudium et Spes*, no. 44, in W. M. Abbott, ed., *The Documents of Vatican II* (New York: America Press, 1966), p. 246. For example, the members of the Woodstock Center for Theological Reflection at Georgetown University, Washington, D.C. serve this distinct purpose.

15. The Stanley Foundation, *op. cit.*, p. 4, 5.

Chapter 8—FAITH AND GLORY

1. "Glory," *Dictionary of Biblical Theology*, Xavier Léon-Duford, S.J., ed., Tr. under P.J. Cahill, S.J. (New York: Desclée Co., 1967), p. 179.

2. *The Shape of the Church to Come*. (New York: Seabury, 1974), p. 86.

3. Hans von Balthasar, *Love Alone*. (New York: Herder and Herder, 1969), p. 48.

4. e.g., "Theological and Pastoral Orientations on the Catholic Charismatic Renewal," Malines, Belgium, May 21-26, 1974. Available: Communications Center, Drawer A, Notre Dame, Ind. 46556. "When the Spirit Moves . . . ", Statement of U.S. Bishops' Committee for Pastoral Research and Practices, *Origins* 4 (1975) 499-502. In the context of ecumenism, A. Dulles, "Now That The Honeymoon is Over," *Origins* 3 (1974) 653,654. *Catholic Pentecostalism: Problems in Evaluation*, Kiliam

McDonnell, O.S.B. Pecos, N.M.: Dove, 1970. *Pentecostalism*, A Theological Viewpoint, Donald L. Gelpi, S.J. New York: Paulist, 1971.

5. *The Text of The Spiritual Exercises of Saint Ignatius.* *op. cit.* p. 73.

6. "Decree on the Ministry and Life of Priests," no. 2 in Abbott, *op. cit.*, p. 536.

7. Dietrich Bonhoeffer as quoted in "God, Ugliness and Beauty," John Drury. *Theology*, October '73, King's College, London, p. 534.

8. Rahner, *Ibid.*, p. 87.

9. Albert-Marie Besnard, O.P., "Tendencies of Contemporary Spirituality." *Concilium*, 9 (New York: Paulist Press, 1966), p. 34.

10. Avery Dulles, S.J., "The Theology of Revelation," *The New Catholic Encyclopedia*, 12 (New York: McGraw-Hill 1967), p. 443.

11. Prof. Reginald Fuller, homilist, Holy Trinity Church, Washington, D.C. February 23, 1975.

12. *Vocubalaire de Théologie Biblique*, Dir. Xavier Léon-Dufour. (Paris: Les Editions du Cerf, 1962). p. 935. (Tr. author).

ADDITIONAL SOURCES:

BOOKS:

Adult Baptism and Catechumenate, Concilium 22. New York: Paulist Press, 1967.

Baum, Gregory, *Man Becoming*. New York: Herder and Herder, 1970.

Bonhoeffer, Dietrich, *Christ The Center*. Tr. John Bowden. New York: Harper & Row, 1960.

Congar, Yves, *Christians Active in the World*. Tr. P. J. Hepburne-Scott. New York: Herder and Herder, 1968.

Cooke, Bernard, S.J., *The Eucharist*. Dayton: Pflaum-Witness Book, 1969.

D'Arcy, Martin C., S.J., *The Mass and the Redemption*. London: Burns Oates and Washbourne, Ltd., 1926.

Dulles, Avery, S.J., *The Dimensions of the Church*. Westminster, Md.: Newman, 1967.

——————— , *Models of the Church*. New York: Doubleday, 1974.

Guitton, Jean, *The Church and the Laity*. Staten Island, N.Y.; Alba House, 1965.

Haughey, John C., *The Conspiracy of God*. New York: Doubleday, 1973.

Lash, Nicholas, *His Presence in the World*. Dayton, Pflaum, 1968.

Ligon, Ernest M., *Dimensions of Character*. New York: Macmillan, 1956.

Marcel, Gabriel, *Men Against Humanity*. London: The Harvill Press, Ltd., 1952.

_____, *The Decline of Wisdom*. New York: Philosophical Library, 1955.

Maslow, A. H. *Motivation and Personality*. New York: Harper and Row, 1954.

McGoldrick, Patrick, ed. *Understanding the Eucharist*. Dublin: Gill and Macmillan, 1969.

Nédoncelle, Maurice. *Love and The Person*. Tr. Sr. Ruth Adelaide, S.C. New York: Sheed and Ward, 1966.

O'Shea, William J., *Sacraments of Initiation*. Englewood Cliffs, N.J.: Prentice-Hall, Inc., 1966.

Polanyi, Michael, *Science, Faith and Society*. Chicago: University of Chicago, 1946.

_____, *The Study of Man*. Chicago: University of Chicago, 1959.

_____, *The Tacit Dimension*. New York: Doubleday-Anchor, 1966.

Pope John XXIII, *Journal of a Soul*. New York: McGraw-Hill, 1964.

Powers, Joseph M., S.J., *Eucharistic Theology*. New York: Herder & Herder, 1967.

Rahner, Hugo, S.J., *The Spirituality of St. Ignatius Loyola*. Tr. Francis John Smith, S.J. Westminster, Md., Newman, 1953.

Rahner, Karl, S.J., *Belief Today*. New York: Sheed and Ward, 1967.

—————, *The Dynamic Element in the Church*. New York: Herder and Herder, 1964.

—————, "Experiencing Easter," *Theological Investigations* VII (New York: Herder & Herder, 1971) 159-168.

—————, "Notes on the Lay Apostolate," *Theological Investigations* II (Baltimore: Helicon, 1971) 319-352.

Spirituality in the Church and World. Concilium 9. New York: Paulist Press, 1965.

Spirituality in the Secular City. Concilium 19. New York: Paulist Press, 1966.

Swanston, Hamish, with Paul and Penny Burns, *Jesus Now*. Vols. 1 & 2, London: Darton, Longman & Todd, 1968.

Teilhard de Chardin, Pierre, *Letters from a Traveler*. New York: Harper & Bros., 1962.

The Resurrection of the Body, H. Cornelius, O.P., J. Guillet, S.J., Th. Camelot. O.P., M.A. Genevois, O.P., Tr. Sr. M. Joselyn, O.S.B. Notre Dame, Ind.: Fides, 1964.

The Spirit of St. Ignatius, Tr. from French by Father Xavier de Franciosi, S.J. New York: Benziger Bros., 1892.

Vogel, Arthur A., *Is the Last Supper Finished: Secular Light on a Sacred Meal*. New York: Sheed and Ward, 1968.

Whelan, Joseph P., *The Spirituality of Friedrich Von Hugel*. London: Collins, 1971.

Woods, Joseph E., *The Spiritual Directory of St. Francis de Sales for People Living in the World.* Westminster, Md.: Newman, 1959.

ARTICLES:

Albertson, Peter D. "Our Badly Educated Clergy." *Parade* supplement, Oct. 25, 1964, pp. 6, 7.

Branson, Roy, "And Now . . . The Theology of Joy," *Encounter*, 34 (1973) 233-245.

Clarke, Thomas E., S.J.,   "The World is Already Christic," *America* 122 (1965) 800-803.

Coventry, John, S.J., "Visible Unity: An Interview with Cardinal Suenens," *One in Christ* 8 (1972) 336-44.

Dougherty, Denis, O.S.B., "The Meaning of the Individual: A Psychological-Theological Pursuit," *The American Benedictine Review* XXIV (1973) 313-326.

Dulles, Avery, S.J., "The Apostolate of Theological Reflection," *The Way* Supplement 20 (1973) 114-123.

_____, "The Church is Communication," *Catholic Mind* LXIX (1971) 6-16.

_____, "The Contemporary Magisterium," *Theology Digest* XVII (1969) 298-311.

Erikson, Rev. Richard C., "The Vulnerable Hero: Theology and the Goals of Therapy," *Journal of Religion and Health*, 12 (1973) 328-336.

Francoeur, Robert T., "The Cosmic Christianity of Teilhard de Chardin," *The Sign* 46 (1967) 8-14.

McManus, Rev. Frederick R., "God's Spirit Works in Lay Words and Deed," *The Tablet* (6/24/1965) 13.

McCormick, Richard A., "The New Morality," *America*, 125 (1968) 769-772.

Meany, John O., "Psychology of 'Personal Theology' and Prayer," *Lumen Vitae* XXVIII (1973) 340-350.

Meyer, Bernard F., M.M., "Catholic Education and the Christian in Society," *Maryknoll* (1962) 20-25.

Pfeiffer, Carl. J., S.J., "How Do I Know What God Wants," *Catholic News* (11/4/71).

Pope Paul VI to Council of the Laity, "The Laity's Mission in the Earthly City," *The Pope Speaks* 17 (1972) 253-256.

Rockower, Isabel, "When You Face a Difficult Decision," *Woman's Day* (Nov. 1969) 20, 126, 127.

Suenens, Cardinal, "Toward Tomorrow's Church," *Catholic Mind* LXX (1972) 11-24.

Thompson, William, "Johannes Metz on the Discernment of Evil," *The American Benedictine Review* XXIV (1973) 473-477.

Toner, Jules J., S.J., "A Method for Communal Discernment of God's Will," *Studies in the Spirituality of Jesuits* 3 (1971) 121-152.

Wild, Robert, "Office and Charisma," *The American Ecclesiastical Review* 167 (1973) 275-283.

Woodrow, Alain, "Discernment and Responsibility," (Editorial) *Uniapac International* 1 (1971) 7.

OTHER:

Dulles, Avery, S.J., "Catholic Theology and the Secondary School." Address delivered Xavier High School, New York City, 12/16/72. Reprinted by Jesuit Secondary Education Association, 1717 Massachusetts Ave., N.W., Washington, D.C.

"Eucharistic Bulletins," The People's Eucharistic League, 194 East 76th Street, N.Y. 10021.

Vanistendael, August, "The Secularization of Life and The Emergence of the Laity." Address to Interfederal Assembly of Pax Romana, Washington, D.C., 2/23/64.